D0007353

POLITICAL LEADERSHIP IN AFRICA

Hoover Institution Studies: 18

POLITICAL LEADERSHIP IN AFRICA

Post-Independence Generational Conflict in Upper Volta, Senegal, Niger, Dahomey, and the Central African Republic

BY VICTOR T. LE VINE

THE HOOVER INSTITUTION
ON WAR, REVOLUTION
AND PEACE
STANFORD UNIVERSITY, 1967

The Hoover Institution on War, Revolution and Peace, founded at Stanford University in 1919 by the late President Herbert Hoover, is a center for advanced study and research on public and international affairs in the twentieth century. The views expressed in its publications are entirely those of the authors and do not necessarily reflect the views of the Hoover Institution.

Library of Congress Catalog Card Number: 67-25788
Printed in the United States of America

ACKNOWLEDGEMENTS

The field research on which this study is based was made possible by a Ford Foundation grant for international studies to Washington University, St. Louis, and by a grant from the Hoover Institution, Stanford University. John Kautsky, Lewis Edinger, and J. David Singer read an earlier version of this paper and offered some highly constructive criticisms and comments. I am grateful for their help, as I am for the suggestions and editorial assistance of Peter Duignan and his colleagues at the Hoover Institution.

CONTENTS

INTRODUCTION

Political leadership in most independent African states is still in the hands of a generation of "elder statesmen"--men who carried the fight against colonialism, who founded the principal political parties, and who developed nationalist ideologies and doctrines. These are men whose backgrounds, political styles, and ideological commitments often seem more appropriate to the winning of independence than to its consolidation or to the establishment of a legitimized political order. Theirs is also the generation of many middle-level administrative cadres, formed by and under the colonial system, whose members profited by their privileged status to move into positions of authority as the colonial powers disengaged themselves from their dependencies.

At the same time a new generation of leaders--usually a group of men who have become politically important since independence--is concerned with the attainment of political goals much different from those that constituted the horizons of the older generation: instead of independence, the elimination of the foreign presence, and greater measures of political freedom and participation, the newer goals are more directly relevant to the post-independence situation--various kinds of economic development, the establishment of effective central government, and the satisfaction of specific political, economic, and social demands. Further, independence has meant a shift in the forms of political action, from agitation against government to its defense, from uncompromising opposition to accommodation, and from the "mobilization and maximization of grievances to their containment, sublimation, or projection onto some new internal or external enemy."[1] In such circumstances, it is a very real question whether leaders of the old generation can effectively shift their behavior and outlook to cope with the demands of the post-revolutionary situation.

It is, then, in the real (or perceived) differences between the older and younger generations, with respect to the fact of independence, that conflict often arises between them. The attitudes of the older leaders, the demands of the younger, and the intensity of the generational conflict, will undoubtedly play a vital role in the future of most of the political systems controlled by Africans. Study of major leadership groups in selected African nations--to glean their members' attitudes, values, and perceptions of their present and future roles--can provide useful descriptive data on current politics in these countries.

This report presents and analyzes data gathered during a five-month research tour in French-speaking west and equatorial Africa (January-June, 1965), focusing on the problems of leadership transition and generational conflict. A total of sixty-eight intensive interviews, including sixty-three self-administered questionnaire sets, was taken in five states: Senegal, Upper Volta, Niger, Dahomey, and the Central African Republic.[2]

The respondents were drawn from occupational categories that represented some of the most important political constituencies in the modern sector of their countries. About a third were drawn from both senior and junior ranks of the civil service. Included in the remainder were ten legislators, eight educators, six high-ranking members of national governments, five lawyers, four labor leaders, three journalists, three businessmen, two military officers, and four others involved in research and voluntary organizations. About half of the respondents were in responsible positions in their countries' dominant political parties. The age range ran from twenty-five to sixty, with most of the respondents (forty-four) in their thirties and forties. Their educational backgrounds ranged from a handful who had completed only primary schooling to a number with advanced or professional university degrees. Most of the respondents were quite well off economically, compared with the bulk of their compatriots, earning substantial salaries and in some instances deriving high additional incomes from investments outside their primary occupations.[*]

[*] A more detailed breakdown of these descriptive data is in Appendix A. For a discussion of the research tools and other methodological considerations, see Appendix B.

I.

GENERAL CONSIDERATIONS

A. The Elite Political Culture in French-speaking Africa

There is no lack of documentation for the proposition that the colonial period in Africa produced several trans-territorial political cultures that survived the transition to independence and that continue to affect the internal and external politics of the post-colonial African states.[3] These transterritorial cultures are modern rather than traditional in the sense that their participants are mainly the products of the Westernized strata of African society. They are elite political cultures involving only a small proportion of Africans, most of whom occupy positions of influence, and excluding the politically unsophisticated African masses. These elite cultures rest upon shared political values, common or similar political experiences, common educational backgrounds, shared nationalist symbols,[4] and, of course, common languages that facilitated the sharing of experiences and ideas before independence and permit political and economic cooperation today. The English-speaking leaders of former British West African colonies are most certainly involved in such a culture, as are those of former British East African dependencies. Whatever may happen to divide them, many of the top leaders of Sierra Leone, Ghana, and Nigeria share the experience of political combat against a common colonial enemy and the common linguistic, political, legal, and cultural legacies left them by Britain. They share many of these things with the top leadership in Kenya, Uganda, Tanzania, and Zambia, who in turn share the experiences that their proximity and pre-independence contacts gave them. Even more clearly delineated and continuously visible is the elite political culture of French-speaking west and equatorial Africa, involving the political elites of Senegal, Mauritania, Guinea, Upper Volta, Niger, Togo, Dahomey, Cameroun, Chad, Central African Republic, Congo/Brazzaville, and Gabon. Geographically marginal, but nonetheless similarly involved, are the leaders of the Malagasy Republic.

The elite political culture of French-speaking Africa ramifies widely and with great complexity within the specific territories, but its salient characteristics can be suggested under five main rubrics:

1. Common French educational experience: training and education in local and metropolitan French schools, seminaries, universities, etc. The seminal role of the École Normale William Ponty, near Dakar, in schooling what was virtually an entire generation of African leaders needs little elaboration.[5] Nor is it necessary to describe the impact of French metropolitan universities and schools attended by French-speaking Africans after 1947;

the contemporary generation of African university students in France is no less affected. It was a common educational culture, for example, that permitted J. P. N'Diaye to assume generalizable results from his questionnaire survey of 294 African students in France in 1961.[6]

2. Shared political values:[7] a high degree of individualism, beliefs in both the efficacy of government as a rational structure and its untrustworthiness as a moral agent; ideologizing on a left-right continuum--on the European model--with particular value attached to the ideologies of the left; achievement (especially education and success in the political arena) viewed as ascriptive in character.

3. Common political education: (for those who emerged in leadership positions before independence) participation in post-war French and French-sponsored political structures such as the National Assembly, Council of the Republic, Senate and Assembly of the French Community, local African legislatures (after 1947), and councils of government (after 1957), and the French bureaucracy.

4. Contact with or participation in French political parties and/or trade unions, or their African affiliates. The first political parties _qua_ political parties that gave French-speaking Africans the possibility of organized political action were the Rassemblement du Peuple Francais (RPF), the Mouvement Républicain Populaires (MRP), the Communist Party of France (PCF), and the French Socialist Party (SFIO), all of which entered the African field once it became possible to compete for seats in the local legislatures

created after October, 1946. Not only were French-speaking Africans involved in these parties in Africa itself, but those who went to France as representatives to metropolitan legislative organs became affiliated or <u>apparenté</u> to parties and groups in France. After 1944, such metropolitan trade unions as the Confédération Générale du Travail (CGT), Confédération Française des Travailleurs Chrétiens (CFTC), and the CGT-Force Ouvrière engaged numerous politically active Africans.[8] Several nationalist parties, in fact, were outgrowths of trade unions or drew cadre from among trade union leadership groups.

5. Involvement in or participation in transterritorial African political parties, movements, and associations. The Rassemblement Démocratique Africain (RDA, founded in 1946), with local branches in Dahomey, Guinea, Ivory Coast, Niger, Senegal, Soudan (now Mali), and Upper Volta, was the first of six such groupings and was prototypical of them all in organization and political style, if not in program or ideology.[9] Though the Niger, Upper Voltan, and Ivory Coast branches are the only ones still nominally affiliated with the RDA, the old RDA tie continues to have great sentimental--and occasionally, practical--value to members of the older generation of African politicians.[10]

The above generalizations do not, of course, apply equally to all participants in the French-speaking African elite political culture; statements three, four, and five, describe for the most part those members of the elite who emerged prior to the independence of their several countries.

All five, however, represent the bases of the elite culture insofar as they represent the common heritage of its members, whatever their ages.

B. Assumptions and Hypotheses

Given the existence of an elite political culture in French-speaking Africa, a number of interesting questions can be raised about it. Apart from the basic ones, such as those concerning the extent of membership, the values of its members, their social background, etc., one of the most interesting is a set involving the impact of independence (i.e., the fulfillment of what can be considered the most important of nationalist goals) upon the values, the behavior, and the expectations of that membership. It was this set of problems that represented the broad context for this study of the passage of power from one generation of leaders to another.

The phenomenon of generational continuity is universal: a society insures its survival by socializing its youth into the values and roles which are functional to the society's activities, and thereby assures its continuity. Generational discontinuity, or more commonly generational conflict, usually occurs when such conflict is itself institutionalized,[11] or when the society is changing more rapidly than its capacity to adapt permits.[12] In Africa, particularly in French-speaking Africa, conditions of rapid political change exist and have existed for some time. One consequence has been that the attitudes, values, and particularly the life experiences of successive generations of leaders have been very different.[13] One of the purposes of this study has been to suggest the nature of those differences, particularly as they relate to the central fact of recent African history; that is, to political independence.

In short, this study seeks evidence on three sets of hypotheses:

1. Independence (as a state of affairs, as a goal, as a political symbol) has affected the values, behaviors, and the expectations of the political elite of French-speaking Africa. For members of the elite in government, for example, it has meant forming new sets of priorities with respect to the allocation of scarce human and financial resources for social and economic development. The governmental elite, given the new priorities, has also had to consider whether changes in political organization were necessary in order to mobilize their societies to the fulfillment of the new goals. Further, independence is no longer a relevant goal for political action; its value as a symbol for political mobilization has been sharply devalued with its attainment. In short, independence now represents an almost totally new political context within which the political elite must seek appropriate modes of expression and behavior.

2. In addition to the usual chronological political generations--which, in some places such as Senegal, are three or even four generations deep--two <u>non-chronological</u> political generations are visible today: a "first" generation

composed of individuals who began their political careers before their countries achieved independence, and who, by and large, arrived at the leadership positions which most of them still hold before that time; and a "second" generation, composed of individuals whose political careers are relatively recent and who arrived at their present positions shortly before or after independence.

3. Some variety of conflict between these two generations exists in French-speaking Africa, and its nature can be ascertained by empirical means. It is further proposed that forms of generational conflict were involved--sometimes crucially--in recent manifestations of political instability and/or violence in some of these countries.

The genesis of the two generations and the historical context of their conflict can also briefly be summarized as part of the background for this study.

The period between 1946 and 1960, in the French-speaking African territories, may be roughly delimited as the era during which agitational politics--aimed at the fulfillment of relatively narrowly conceived nationalist goals--involved most of the African leaders. Many of these leaders, to be sure, began to think of independence seriously only after 1958. Houphouet-Boigny, Lamine Gueye, and Senghor, among many others, are cases in point.[14] Yet insofar as such leaders were concerned with the creation of <u>African</u> political parties, with the search for increased <u>African</u> political participation, and with the quest for greater

African territorial political autonomy, it can be said at least that their goals were quasi-nationalist in character. In any case, agitational politics was for them, as well as for those who had made independence their goal much earlier, the accepted mode of political expression. The available evidence suggests that that leadership arose from extremely varied cultural, educational, and professional circumstances. Conditioned at first to operating within the framework of oppositional politics, those leaders brought to the governing of their respective states skills, commitments, orientations shaped by long experience of agitation and opposition. Many of these first generation leaders (particularly those active in the old RDA and the immediate postwar era) are now middle-aged--indeed jaded--and almost all are beginning to be faced with problems accompanying the rise and challenge of a generation of younger men. Most of them (with reservations, of course) are better educated than their mentors; most of them have less political skill but greater technical expertise in such areas as administration, finance, economics, and law, and most of them have fewer francophilic commitments. The passing of the older--if just in terms of having acquired its experience before independence--generation of the political elite in the French-speaking states, will come to have profound repercussions on the internal and external politics of these states.

II.

WHAT IS THE AFRICAN ELITE? WHO ARE THE AFRICAN ELITE?

One of the better definitions of the term "elite" is that of S. F. Nadel, advanced in his analysis of "The Concept of Social Elites." He concludes that an elite is an aggregate of people with distinct characteristics: a position of high status; some degree of corporate group character as well as exclusiveness; awareness of their preeminent position as the consequence of some attribute which they share by right; recognition of their general superiority by the society at large; and imitability--"the elite, by its very manner of acting and thinking, sets the standards for the whole society, its influence or power being that of a model accepted and considered worth following."[15] Nadel's definition is excellent, insofar as it includes and describes all those individuals who occupy top positions in a society. However, it does not distinguish between what Pareto called the governing and the non-governing elite; that is, between those "who directly or indirectly play some considerable part in the government" and those who do not.[16] The definitional problem is complicated by the fact that there are two dichotomized, related ways of identifying elites: (1) objectively-subjectively, that is, by the application of external criteria or by the application of criteria suggested by both elites and non-elites; (2) by the use of either situational or reputational criteria, that is, by stipulating what social offices, positions, roles are "elite" in nature, then arbitrarily ascribing "elite" character to those occupying them, or by asking members of a society to name "elite" positions and those whom they deem as being of the "elite." For the purpose of this study, both situational and reputational criteria were utilized in the selection of respondents. "French-speaking African political elite," therefore, refers to all those persons "who because of their education, social position, occupation, economic power consider themselves elites and thereby lay claim more or less effectively, to political power."[17] Included are "the people of the Establishment,"[18] that is, persons occupying formal positions of political power, whether or not they or others consider them as members of the elite or as wielding political power.

The definitional problem is not, it must be added, merely an academic one, nor simply one that had to be solved in some reasonable manner so that respondents for this study might be selected. The term, with all its ambiguities, has entered the colloquial language of French-speaking Africa, and has come to be used in a variety of contexts and connections having little to do with the more specific formulations of scholars. Secondary-school students consider themselves part of the "elite"; village chiefs refer to themselves as members of the "traditional elite," and African push-cart vendors in Yaoundé (contemptuously dismissed as margoulins* by their better-off Levantine competitors) spoke seriously of being part of the urban commercial "elite." So did the Levantine traders, for that matter.[19] However the term is used, it refers to the general superiority of one group (usually one's own) over another or others. And, when the term is used by those individuals who can be objectively described as being of the political elite, some exploration of its meaning with these individuals can evoke highly revealing clues about basic political values and attitudes.

In the expectation that evidence of generational conflict might be adduced from differing responses to the definitional problem, the interviewees were asked, during the oral interview, to define "African elite." Once a response had been given, and if they had not themselves made the connection, the subjects were then asked to what extent their definition applied to their own country. Related to this open-ended discussion, were four items in Questionnaire 2, designed to elicit peer nominations, with implicit ranking scales in each question. The interview and questionnaire responses were constructed to obtain indications of (a) the way in which elites viewed eliteness, (b) how elites viewed the elite constituency, i.e., definitions of the eligibility parameters, (c) whether the respondents' perceptions and images of the elite were consonant with his peer nominations; whether there existed congruence between his definition of

---

*Bagmen, dealers of cheap, shoddy wares.

the elite and the actual characteristics of those he nominated as representative of the elite.

The response to the definition question varied considerably, but one important distinction emerged: most of the first-generation elite tended to feel that some form of "activism" was the prime characteristic of the elite, while most of those in the second generation stressed the possession of formal education as the main feature of eliteness. The first generation respondents stressed the point that formal education was not in and of itself sufficient to qualify individuals for elite status; it was obviously desirable, but to define the elite in such narrow terms was to miss the facts of the present situation. The elite, in that view, included people from all walks of life, individuals who had had some sort of "calling" (the term _prise de conscience_ occurred sixteen times in the interviews) to serve, to lead, their people. "Experience," "active participation" in the country's political affairs, "doing, not thinking," were representative expressions that conveyed this point of view. The doers, the activists, the actual occupants of leadership positions--these were the elite, and they might include not only ministers in government, but traditional chiefs who had experienced the _prise de conscience_ and dedicated themselves to the advancement of their country. Most of the second-generation respondents considered education to be the hallmark of eliteness. One respondent (civil servant, age thirty-three) put it thus: "Education now confers a privilege previously unknown; the educated are a social group with similar views and affinities, and their intellectual achievement gives them an understanding of their country's problems unavailable to others." The elite, according to at least ten second-generation respondents, were people "with a certain culture;" others in the category spoke of those "who were not simply holding down positions because of age or family connections," of those who brought "modern skills" to the nation, of those who were concerned with solving the immediate (emphasis on immediate) problems of their country.

Only a relatively small proportion of the respondents--most of them, significantly, people holding professional positions, such as doctors, lawyers, educators in institutions of higher learning--provided definitions that either failed to make the above distinction or acknowledged the distinction, but deprecated it. Nine respondents fell into this category; they tended to see the elite in relatively broad terms, as extending to all classes of society, as open to anyone demonstrating leadership, be it because of educational, activist, or other achievement criteria. One Senegalese even suggested that "elite" was "a chimerical term" that forced unnecessary distinctions.

The definitions, seen in perspective, represented in most cases defenses of the respondents and their claim to exclusiveness. No respondent questioned the fact that he or she was in fact a member of the elite and hence qualified to lead. All the respondents who replied to the definitional question (sixty-five) stressed achievement rather than ascriptive criteria in their view of what constituted eliteness and the parameters of elegibility. Fifty of the respondents, however, tended to see their own and their peers' achievements as conferring ascriptive qualities: the "right" to rule, the "privilege" of leadership, the "duty of service." Achievement, according to them, was relatively unrestricted, be it by education, activism, _prise de conscience_, call to leadership, etc., but once one _had_ achieved, one had become, as it were, a member of a meritocracy. Having reached, or been drawn into this aristocracy of achievement, a certain (though none used the phrase) noblesse oblige was incumbent.

The peer-nomination questions produced some interesting and somewhat unanticipated results. Eighteen respondents either wrote in their refusal to answer the questions or left the spaces blank. Of the forty-five who did reply, all replied to the "African leaders" question (Questionnaire 2, No. 5); forty-one replied to both No. 5 and the local nomination questions (Questionnaire 2, Nos. 7, 8). Most did not nominate more than three leaders. The actual nominations made in the three questions were not surprising: the "African leaders" were those generally in the news (Houphouet-Boigny, Senghor, Sekou Toure, Nkrumah were mentioned most frequently), and the local nominations were almost invariably headed by the local president, his cabinet, the national assembly president, and usually included those persons occupying the highest formal offices in the government, the leading political party, and so forth. What was unexpected was the difference between most of the respondents' definitions of the elite and the actual nominations they made. The difference was clearest with respect to the second-generation elites and their local nominations: almost all of those in this category who responded to the nomination questions simply gave names of individuals occupying formal positions of power, whether or not they had in fact the criteria of eliteness specified by the respondents. Even those of the second generation who saw their elders in the most negative terms failed to apply these views to their nominations. Some of the Senegalese second-generation respondents, for example, named the Grand Marabout of the Mouride sect, El Hadj Falilou M'backé, as the second most influential Senegalese, though they denied in the oral interview that traditional chiefs were members of the elite. Why the dichotomy between definition and nomination? One reason may have been the form of the nomination questions; the local nominations were to be "the most influential persons," and it would appear that to the respondents who gave incongruent answers, those whom they identified as influential were simply that, and not necessarily members of the "elite." The conversations revealed that the respondents did not see any necessary correlation between membership in the elite and the wielding of political influence. This conclusion, though tentative, is partially borne out by the answers to the questionnaire's efficacy series (Questionnaire 2, No. 13), in which most respondents tended to minimize, even deny their own abilities to affect governmental decisions.

The "African leaders" nominations are reported below (see table) (Questionnaire 2, No. 5): "During the next five years, who are the African leaders, who, in your opinion, will play the most important roles in inter-African politics? (Indicate by No. 1 the most important; No. 2, the second, etc.)"

Number of Nominations	Leaders	Rankings and Frequencies 1	2	3	4	5	6	7	8	9	10
40	Houphouet-Boigny	17	16	5	2	0	0	0	0	0	0
30	Senghor	9	9	8	4	0	0	0	0	0	0
19	S. Touré	1	5	2	6	3	1	1	0	0	0
15	Nkrumah	4	2	6	0	2	1	0	0	0	0
13	Ben Bella	3	2	2	3	2	0	1	0	0	0
13	Nasser	2	2	3	1	3	1	0	0	0	1
11	M. Keita	2	2	4	2	1	0	0	0	0	0
10	H. Diori	3	6	1	0	0	0	0	0	0	0
10	Bourguiba	0	0	3	3	4	0	0	0	0	0
8	Kenyatta	1	1	1	0	2	3	0	0	0	0
6	Abubakar T. Balewa	1	0	2	2	0	1	0	1	0	0
5	H. Selassie	2	0	1	1	0	1	0	0	0	0
5	Ahidjo	0	0	2	1	0	0	2	0	0	0
4	Tsiranana	0	0	2	1	0	1	0	0	0	0
4	M. Yameogo	0	0	1	0	1	1	1	1	0	0
3	Tshombe	0	0	0	0	2	0	0	0	1	0
18	No Response										

III.

THE GENERATIONS VIEW EACH OTHER: PARTICIPATION, GOALS, ACHIEVEMENT

The five countries selected for this study shared, at the time of this study, at least one common denominator: they were either one-party or one-party-dominant systems. In Senegal, the Bloc Démocratique Sénégalais (BDS), party of Senghor and Lamine Gueye, dominates the political scene, with opposition groups such as the Parti Africain d'Indépendance (PAI) in formal proscription. In Upper Volta, the Union Démocratique Voltaique (UDV) was the sole legal party; the Parti Populaire Nigerien (PPN) enjoys similar status in Niger, as did the Mouvement d'Evolution Sociale d'Afrique Noire (MESAN) in the Central African Republic. In Dahomey, the Parti Populaire Dahoméen (PPD) dominated politics. In each country, the official party-governmental line had repeatedly stressed the desirability, even necessity of increased political participation by "the people," and in particular by the elite, to the ends of national construction. To most top African leaders, the elite must not only participate, but must become wholly involved--*engagé*--as active members of the dominant party. Only when this occurs can the governing parties effectively mobilize national human and physical resources.[20] The problem of securing such involvement-participation seemed therefore to offer another promising opening onto the problem of generational conflict, and all of the respondents who permitted the oral interview were asked their views on the subject. Given the open-end nature of the interviews and the varied political situations in each country, phrasing of the questions differed somewhat, but each respondent was asked to focus on the involvement of young people, particularly those returned or returning from studies abroad, in their country's political life. Subsequent exploratory questions mentioned the dominant party, or one of the organizations associated or connected with it.

Inasmuch as the responses tended to vary according to country, and before suggesting some overall patterns that emerged from the discussions in this area, it may be useful to consider each country separately.

1. Senegal

Throughout much of Africa, a severe shortage of trained, educated persons hampers political and economic development. It has been wryly suggested that in Senegal and Dahomey, it is a surplus of educated people that most retards development. The charge contains some elements of truth, particularly as it applies to Senegal. The Senegalese elite has been admirably described elsewhere,[21] so there is no need to do so here, save to point out that the nation has long contained an unusually high number of well educated people, many from families with established traditions of educational achievement. These include not only graduates from William Ponty and Senegalese _lycées_ and technical schools, but university graduates as well. The exceptional nature of the Senegalese situation is described by Professor Ruth Schachter Morgenthau:

> In French, unlike British West Africa, there existed almost no university graduates in 1945. The handful of exceptions came almost exclusively from Senegal, and primarily there from among the pre-war 'citizens' living in Dakar, Saint-Louis, Rufisque, and Gorée. Only among this comparatively privileged community could some select families point to as many as three generations of educated men. Among the 'citizens' most who had acquired pre-war French university degrees were trained as veterinary surgeons--for example the novelist and Socialist mayor of Rufisque, Ousmane Soce Diop. The grammarian and poet, Leopold Senghor, and the doctor of law, Me Lamine Gueye--both naturalized pre-war 'citizens'--were also among the Senegalese exceptions.[22]

The coming of independence saw Senegal endowed with a highly Africanized civil service composed of men whose educational achievements were usually several notches above Africans in other countries occupying similar positions. In 1965, more than forty percent of the total salaried labor force--over 40,000 of about 100,000 persons--were employed by government, and places in the administrative governmental establishment, preferred by university and secondary-school graduates, had become increasingly difficult to secure. There was, by 1965, a large and ever-growing population of what Senegalese themselves described as "surplus intellectuals." These individuals, graduates of Senegalese, French-speaking African, and French secondary (and some higher) institutions, clamor at the governmental gates, and comprise something of a disaffected, disillusioned class.[23]

The nine second-generation respondents of the fifteen Senegalese interviewees, insofar as they occupied desirable positions (two civil servants, two newspaper editors, two legislators, two teachers, and a magistrate) could lay claim to having solved the problem of finding work suitable to their talents, but shared--according to their statements--some of the values of the "surplus" intellectuals and indeed, by their own references, identified with them to a considerable extent. They tended to see the first-generation leaders as part of a relatively closed corporation--relatively, since the government had begun to fill the so-called "technical" ministries (Education, Finance, Justice, Economic Development) with persons possessing the requisite technical skills. Yet, the positions of "real" power were occupied by _les anciens_: the old party leaders, the grand _marabouts_, members of the old _assimilé_ families, the Catholic monied, the big businessmen. The party operated to restrict the entrance of younger people to real influence. (A member of the UPS[*]

---

[*]Union Progressiste Sénégalaise, the governing party of Senegal, founded in 1958.

executive committee admitted to the interviewer that the party chiefs were not generally concerned with bringing young blood into the party, and in fact, "they are usually ignored.") Politics, defined as active participation in the UPS, did not, to the second generation respondents, constitute a promising area of involvement. In the striking metaphor of a young civil servant, politics was "a basket of crabs" into which no sensible person would thrust his fingers. The party, according to another respondent, was more of a brake than a help to personal advancement. Several spoke of the consequences that dissidence within the party might entail: loss of job, expulsion from the party, possible imprisonment, reprisals against family, etc.

The second-generation respondents tended, in sum, to see themselves as both shunted aside by their elders and rejecting political activity in favor of "doing their job," "concentrating on their professions," and the like. The educated, returning Senegalese, they agreed almost unanimously, tended to avoid political involvement for one or more of the reasons cited above, and consequently kept away from membership in the UPS. A few did join the UPS, according to two respondents who were the only UPS members in the second-generation group, for reasons of sheer opportunism. Such membership, they assured the interviewer, could not be equated with commitment or "true" involvement. A small percentage of the returnees, unable to restrain their political bent, entered into oppositional politics overtly or clandestinely.

Most of the first-generation respondents readily admitted that younger well educated people stayed away from party involvement in alarming numbers. Four contended that the problem was serious but not critical, since most of the young people, after several years back in the country or in positions of responsibility, joined the party anyway; their integration and involvement would ultimately take place. Two felt a certain sympathy with the young people, considering a "certain incompatibility" between the "tasks of the intellectual" and the business of politics. One denied there was a problem, then assailed the "unprincipled opportunists" who entered the party for other than ideologically pure reasons. First-generation respondents tended to agree that the second-generation group included a large number of "impetuous," "unrealistic," "immature" (all adjectives used by respondents) persons. Their long stay abroad caused them to lose touch with political realities at home, and they returned, degrees in hand, expecting the best jobs, the fullest responsibilities, and radical change according to their prescriptions. Two interviewees advanced hypotheses to explain the alleged hostility of the younger for the older generation:

> (Lawyer) "Perhaps what they see as the reality of Senegal and the government's position fails to correspond to their idealism. Or, they simply cannot find the 'right' ("right" pronounced with sarcasm: Interviewer) place for themselves."

(Legislator) "Before independence, politics had the flavor of intrigue, and was for that reason looked down upon by the youth. That flavor lingers for many, many, who are genuinely interested in solving the country's pressing problems. They want to do something, but do not want to do it within the UPS."

2. Upper Volta

Unlike Senegal, Upper Volta appears not to have an "intellectual surplus." Rather, the picture suggests genuine penury in such areas as teachers, trained technicians, engineers, doctors, and in fact in most areas where qualification implies expertise acquired through training. Over 450 French technical assistance personnel work in Upper Volta, including not only those manning slots in the governmental machinery but also fifty-six French teachers fulfilling their military obligations by teaching at the Lycée Ouezzin Coulibaly in Ouagadougou and in other schools.[24] The Yameogo government's policy was to replace expatriates by trained Upper Voltans as soon as these become available, and there is no indication that the post-Yameogo regime is thinking otherwise.

Official manpower-need projections for the period 1961-65 listed 542 positions in government; in March, 1965, only 124 Upper Voltans of the more than 350 abroad in secondary and higher institutions in France and Africa were said to be in training for these positions.[25] An unofficial estimate by persons in the Ministry of Education suggested that it would be at least five to eight years before all the expatriates could be replaced, perhaps ten years before the country's immediate governmental trained personnel needs could be met. The under-employed or unemployed intellectual--whatever the reason for his situation--is not now a source of discontent or an object of identification for young Upper Voltans. Yet, the seven second-generation respondents in the Upper Voltan group (of fifteen interviewees) tended to reflect much the same judgments about political involvement and the same sort of criticisms of "les anciens" in power as did their peers in Senegal. All disparaged participation in the Union Démocratique Voltaique as "sterile," "uninteresting," "unproductive." Even the two who were in fact members of the party explained that they were members not so much by conviction --though they tended to support most of the government's policies--as because their official positions required it. The first generation's leaders were seen as clinging to power and unwilling to permit any changes that might threaten their positions. Some second-generation elite have in fact moved into key governmental positions, but they are seen by "les anciens" as technocrats, and have usually accepted a technical rather than political role in governmental affairs. One conversation with a second-generation labor leader is worth quoting in part, because it epitomizes some of the feeling of his group:

Q. Are youth staying away from politics?

A. The old generation is keeping them away. Before independence, there was a definite enemy to fight; now the lines have become indistinct. In the transition, the old generation is groping, and doesn't want youth to interfere.

Q. In this situation, what do young people do? What can they do?

A. Some want to express their ideas, but discover that they can't. . . . So they have to remain quiet. They feel bottled-up, frustrated. The older generation leaders feel the youth are not ripe, that the youth need more experience before laying claim to leadership.

. . . .

In the party youth have slim chances for advancement, except for those who play the regime's game. Dissidents are quickly isolated. In the present state of things you may get docility, but no new ideas.

Q. What of students who return? It is said that some come back hostile to the regime. Do you agree?

A. Yes. Many youth become radicals <u>after</u> they come back because they are not integrated into the country's elite; because they are not permitted to speak freely. The fact of this lack of integration pushes the youth into radical positions, into opposition to the regime.

Other respondents spoke of the "lack of constructive dialogue" between the country's leaders and the educated youth, complained that "we are to follow uncritically," and one noted derisively, "with all the government's pretensions of socialism, no real socialist could join a party controlled by self-serving politicians." All agreed that the young, well-educated Upper Voltans seemed unwilling to become involved in partisan politics, either because of the risks or because of a basic conflict between their own ideals and the regime's policies.

All but one of the first-generation respondents tended to minimize the participation problem, contending that in one way or another the "young intellectuals" entered public life and full political participation even if at first they avoided political involvement, preferring the anonymity of only bureaucratic tasks. One respondent's reply, partially quoted below, is representative: "This is not an unknown problem here in Upper Volta; but youth, in time, in contact with reality, abandon their distrust (of us). They come to understand that miraculous solutions do not occur simply by willing them." Four of the eight admitted the UDV was having trouble recruiting younger blood. One respondent, a trade-union leader, deputy, and outspoken critic of the regime, stressed the lack of realism he claimed was common to the educated returnees: "Most who come back are in general very ignorant of African life. They may have left while they were quite young; they may have been away too long and come to adopt ways and ideas inappropriate to those in their country. Most have been involved in student activity in the worst sense--communist or radical groups--and they return with ideas far too advanced for their time." He noted, however, that returnees tend to avoid national politics, because in the dominant party, "they have no way of expressing themselves. They must stay in obscurity until the leadership gives them something to do. In such a situation they either hide their true feelings or simply give in." The trade unions, he contended, represented one of the few remaining areas of free political expression, and were hence centers of attraction for educated intellectuals.

3. Niger

The Niger group comprised eighteen individuals, equally divided between first- and second-generation respondents. Their answers reflected, as did those in Upper Volta, the absence of an "intellectual surplus" and a recognition of the relatively broad range of positions open to persons with the requisite skills. They did, however, diverge in their view of the extent to which the political system was open, particularly to younger intellectuals.

On the basis of the Senegalese and Upper Voltan interviews, the answers to the integration-involvement questions appeared relatively predictable. They were, but only up to a certain point. The first-generation respondents almost unanimously expressed agreement that most of the young people who returned to Niger had no trouble finding responsible positions, and that they usually joined either the Parti Populaire Nigerien or its youth wing. Four of this group mentioned the 1964 "Cadre-youth Seminar," citing it as one of the more successful of the government's efforts to provide ample opportunity for youth to question the regime's policies and to take an active part in the country's political life. Two of this group did suggest that perhaps in five years or so--after the jobs currently occupied by Frenchmen were filled by Nigeriens--a problem might arise.

Respondents in the second-generation group varied a good deal in their answers to the questions; only two of them, however, felt that there was no problem at all. The rest expressed various degrees of dissatisfaction with the extent to which youth was in fact integrated and integrating into Niger's political life. For example, four who mentioned the cadre-youth conference agreed that it had not constituted a "real" dialogue, that there was in fact insufficient communication between the country's leaders and its youth. Most felt that they and others like them (even though formally PPN members) were keeping away from active political participation, preferring instead to apply themselves to their jobs and wait until things became (using one respondent's term) "riper" for them. ("Ripeness," when explored by the interviewer, emerged as that time--ascertainable mainly through intuition--when *la relève*, or the changing of the guard, could take place without violence.) Somewhat surprisingly (when compared to the younger elite in Senegal), none in this group of respondents expressed overt opposition to the country's leadership; most, in fact, had words of praise for President Diori and his associates.

4. Dahomey

Dahomey shares with Senegal the acute problems of assimilating a large unemployed or underemployed intellectual elite. Like Senegal, Dahomey has been burdened with a bureaucracy larger than its economy can bear. Virginia Thompson, in 1961, reported 18,298 civil servants on the government payroll;[26] in 1965 that number had increased to about 22,000, and 64.3 percent of the 1964 budget was allocated for government salaries.[27] Unlike Senegal, Dahomey has been faced not only with assimilating students returning from studies abroad, but with absorbing in some manner several thousand functionaries who once filled positions elsewhere in French-speaking Africa, and were sent home after 1958, when locals began demanding their places, or when, with the coming of independence, they became the object of resentment. The anti-Dahomean riots in the Ivory Coast and Niger in 1958 and 1960 are examples in point. Dahomey's first-generation elite includes, then, not only persons occupying strategic positions in the economy and the government, but individuals on the outside looking in who feel they are due the positions to which their experience and training entitles them. This latter group has trained its guns on every regime since independence, and on the younger elite in the positions of authority to which its members feel entitled. The second-generation elite, therefore, has had to bear the crossfire of pressure from its own peers both in and out of influence, from the regime that sought to goad it into open support, and from the unemployed returnees. The sixteen Dahomean interviewees--of whom fourteen completed both questionnaires and interview --not unexpectedly reflected these tensions.

All the Dahomean respondents readily admitted that the regime, in fact every regime in Dahomey, had had the greatest difficulty in integrating its second-generation youth. Ten of the sixteen mentioned the shortage of available governmental positions compared with the number of applicants. Three pointed out that "intellectuals" sought government positions rather than places in business or industry because the private sector was both depressed and dominated by foreigners.

Nine of the respondents identified themselves as belonging to the second generation. All agreed that Dahomean youth have tended to withdraw from politics, that theirs was the attitude of "attentisme," of waiting for the time when their voice can be heard and their influence can be felt. Dahomean politics, in the words of one respondent,

> ...is the politics of personality.... Politics in Dahomey is very dangerous; it is too unstable. Your job is at stake if you speak out. Since most of us are in administration, we manifest a certain prudence. Most of us regard political life as futile, and politicians are looked upon as generally intellectually inferior.... Those who do join the party

> do so not because of conviction, but out of opportunism, out of choice for the material advantages that accompany support of the party in power.

Five of the second generation declared themselves frustrated by the turn of political events in Dahomey brought about by the inability of _les anciens_ to collaborate with the younger intellectuals. There was a time, during the first provisional regime of Colonel Soglo (October, 1963-January, 1964) when a group of young technicians and intellectuals who had helped to create the Soglo coup occupied key positions in government. One of that group, still in government, sounded its keynote--and that of the whole second generation group. What he said is worth quoting extensively:

> In the authoritarian countries of the right (Ivory Coast, Dahomey, Senegal) youth seemed to stay away from politics. They saw themselves as technocrats, and persuaded themselves that politics is a _faux jeu_. . . . So we too, under the old regime, we stood aside. But, we did play an important role in the revolution of October 28 (1963), and the present regime is due to a close collaboration with youth. But after eighteen months, there are some of us who consider ourselves to have been pushed aside. During the provisional regime we hoped and believed in miracles; we hoped that the new rulers could put a new face on the country. What happened? We saw that these leaders were people of a sort different from what we had hoped. They turned out to be a bourgeoisie of _fonctionnaires_ without a sense of initiative, who quickly went back to doing things as they had been done under Maga. . . . So we stayed,

> not because we liked the situation, but because we didn't want to be reproached for not working for our country.

The seven first-generation respondents articulated rather deeply felt grievances against the second generation, expressed varying senses of frustration at the fact they had been left to face the country's problems and indiscriminate sniping from the youth at the same time. "Criticism," said one respondent, "is Dahomey's cheapest commodity, and everyone has wholesale lots to sell or give away freely." "The new generation," according to another, "wants to rule from its air-conditioned offices. They lack contact with the masses and the will to acquire that experience." A third, speaking of the returning students, claimed, "Many of the youth want guarantees--a high wage, housing, a car--before they return. . . . Some have even left, after coming back, disappointed that they weren't getting enough." Politics, to another, was a way of getting people what they wanted--within reason. The younger generation wanted everything at once: jobs, security, reforms, power, and the adulation of the masses and their elders. It was too much.

5. Central African Republic

Since official permission originally granted to conduct this investigation in the CAR was subsequently withdrawn (see methodological appendix), it was impossible to complete the interviews that were begun there. However, the incomplete interviews did reveal some attitudes similar to those encountered in the four other countries.

The formal prohibition against any political groups outside the MESAN, plus an active campaign to bring returning youth and local leaders into the party's youth wing, appeared to have kept at a low level the number of overt CAR *attentistes*. Most second-generation elites had in fact joined MESAN or its youth wing, but there were some complaints that this formal integration had not also resulted in complete commitment or involvement. Some of the respondents spoke of a group of "young Turks," who stood for more radical ideas and programs than the "*vieux turbans*" in control of the party Central Committee and the key governmental positions. The "young Turks," numbering between 50 and 150--depending on the informant--well educated young men, were said to feel that the party and the country's leadership "lacked vigor, determination and dedication." Although apparently there was little problem in getting second-generation elites both good jobs in government and membership in the MESAN--given a shortage of both trained personnel and party militants--generational cleavage did exist within the regime in sufficiently large dimensions that both the "*vieux turbans*" and the "young Turks" (and those who identified with them) felt somewhat threatened by each other.

6. Participation and the Generations: Summary and Analysis

Before any generalizations can be hazarded on the responses to the involvement-participation set of questions, it must be emphasized that the extent to which the respondents' perceptions about themselves or each other corresponded to reality was not crucial to the problem. What was important was the perceptions themselves, the images the two generations had about themselves and each other. Nor was the definition of the two generations in question; the respondents accepted the distinctions implied by the questionnaires and the interview questions. When challenged, references to _les anciens_, _les vieux_, _les jeunes_, _la jeune generation_, and the like, elicited definitions generally corresponding to those set up by the interviewer.

The two generations, to judge from the responses, tended to view each other with considerable distrust. The suspicions of the second generation operationally translated themselves, in most cases, into one of two forms of _attentisme_: a refusal to become involved in the dominant party or in any other party activity, or a pro forma membership in the dominant party without active participation. The second-generation respondents tended to see their elders as lacking understanding (there was frequent reference to the "lack of dialogue" or the fruitlessness of such dialogue), or as clinging to positions of power and restricting entry into the circles of "real" influence to those who submit and play their game. Politics, in the eyes of the second-generation respondents, was seen as "dangerous" or as presenting unacceptable hazards. The younger group appeared to consider themselves technically more competent to solve national problems than their elders, and approved any demonstration that some of their number could use their skills to good advantage, but in general they decried the fact that they were so little consulted or their skills so little utilized. Though most disclaimed any political ambitions as such--three-fourths of this group issued such denials--all appeared to be intensely interested by national politics, and most were willing to talk at length on the subject. They had not, it appeared from their list of associational activities, given up political activity entirely; they joined discussion groups, participated in debates, attended lectures at which they voiced their feelings, or became involved in "cultural" groups of one sort or another in which political talk often constituted the chief activity. Politics became for many a verbal activity one pursued with one's friends. It was this aspect of the second generation's political activities that aroused some of their elders to accuse the younger group of "talking only to themselves" or, worse, of appearing to be engaged in various sorts of conspiracy.

The first-generation respondents for the most part were concerned about the withdrawal of the second generation from active participation in the regime's official party or groups. They felt they had been misunderstood and wrongly judged; above all, they stressed what some termed "the lack of realism" displayed by students, returnees, younger civil servants, and self-styled intellectuals. Many younger men, it was felt, lacked understanding of their country and its problems, due to long absences from home or supercharged idealism. Above all, youth lacked experience, and "all the technical skill in the world" (in the words of a first-generation legislator from Dahomey) could not compensate for that. The members of the younger elite had to serve an apprenticeship before they could be permitted responsibility over people's lives, and their impatience and pressure on their elders made the latter's tasks that much more difficult.

IV.

POLITICAL EFFICACY AND THE GENERATIONS

Political efficacy, as defined by the limited literature on the subject, refers to an individual's perceptions of his ability to effect political (or social) changes in his political (or social) environment. Crucial to the concept is the hypothesis that the individuals' feelings of competence vis-à-vis the political system make a difference in the extent to which people accept or reject it, and ultimately affect the degree of the system's stability.[28] Participation and its allied attitudes, as discussed in the previous section, represent one index of intergenerational conflict. Insofar as participation is related to political efficacy or political competence (and other research seems to indicate that there is a connection), we assumed that if there was a difference between the generations in the manner in which they saw participation as a political desideratum, then ratings of subjective competence ought to reflect that difference. To recapitulate briefly, second-generation respondents saw their peers and themselves as having low levels of formal participation and involvement. The first-generation respondents agreed that such was the case, and in this respect explicitly or implicitly rated themselves highly by comparison. One might have expected, then, a high-level sense of subjective competence from the first-generation respondents, a low level from the second. The results of the efficacy questions (Questionnaire 2, No. 13) were surprising for two reasons: (1) the participation differences were not reflected, and (2) estimates of subjective competence bore little relation to most respondents' actual positions or to their reputation for competent performance.

The questions themselves were adapted from the Almond-Verba questionnaire, and, given the nature of the respondents, were phrased for the national rather than the local political scene.[29] Moreover, there was no preliminary question to explore familiarity with national issues, since all the respondents, as members of their countries' political elite, were assumed to have such familiarity. The interviews confirmed this assumption. Further, the efficacy series were frequently discussed during the interviews at the request of the respondents, and the opportunity for discussion permitted some interesting amplifications on the questions themselves.

Of the sixty-three respondents who completed both questionnaires and interviews, only forty-two answered the efficacy questions. The high number of refusals may have been due to the form of the question, phrased to elicit the respondent's reaction to the national government's acts. Suspicions may have been aroused that the interviewer was trying to discover oppositional attitudes. The refusals divided almost equally between first- and second-generation respondents, but most of the refusals (fifteen) came from persons occupying governmental posts in Upper Volta and Niger. The actual replies divided twenty to twenty-two between second- and first-generation respondents.

Predictably, most of the second-generation respondents rated their subjective competence quite low. What was surprising was that most of the first-generation respondents revealed similar negative self-evaluations. The similarities between the two groups of respondents can be stated in simple terms for the purposes of this preliminary analysis:

(Questionnaire 2, No. 13) "Suppose the national government is considering a law that you judge unjust or pernicious. What do you think you could do about it?"

Replies	First Generation	Second Generation	No. of Respondents
Could do nothing	12	16	28
Could do very little	8	1	9
Could effect some sort of change	2	3	5
			42

In such a situation, what are the chances that you would do something to show your opposition?

Replies	First Generation	Second Generation	No. of Respondents
Chances good, high	10	8	18
Chances poor, none, little	12	10	22
Don't know	2		2
			42

If you do make an effort to change the law, what are the chances that you might be successful in your efforts?

Replies	First Generation	Second Generation	No. of Respondents
Probably success	5	2	7
Little, low, none	13	18	31
Don't know	4		4
			42

The similarity between the two groups' views on efficacy is sufficiently striking to warrant some attempt at explanation. After re-examining the elite definition responses, the interview discussions on the efficacy series, and comments made about the impact of independence on the goals of the respondents, an interesting picture began to emerge.

It appeared that before or at the time of independence, efficacy in the sense of subjective evaluations of ability to manipulate men and events was extremely high for most members of the elite. Independence, or promised independence, represented a visible--though symbolic--payoff for competence. The independence symbol was sufficiently diffuse, it seems, to permit a wide range of people who had made widely different contributions to the attainment of the goal to feel tangibly rewarded for their efforts. It represented, in short, a reward that was concrete enough to be visible and understood, but sufficiently diffuse and undifferentiated to permit its sharing by the greatest number of persons. The sense of efficacy was, then, extremely high during the period immediately preceding and following independence.[30] It was not long, however, before that sense began to decline considerably, and importantly, it declined for men who by positional and reputational criteria were so situated as to be able to effect and enjoy favorable political payoffs. Nearly all the first-generation respondents were such men (see Appendix A). Efficacy, the sense of subjective political competence, declined alike for cabinet ministers, senior functionaries, party leaders, top trade unionists, and intellectuals. Why? Elisabeth Colson, writing about the political competence among the Tonga of Zambia, related competence to performance--to political payoffs in terms of visible changes in the political environment.[31] The Tonga rated competence in relation to personal rewards they garnered through the client-patron relationship that constituted their way of relating to the dominant, extra-Tonga political power. Before independence, a politically competent Tonga was one who used "his" white man to produce tangible benefits. After independence, the Tonga adapted the relationship to the new African rulers who gave them, at least initially, symbolic rewards (independence, deference, a sense of superiority to the white man, etc.) while promising tangible rewards later on. It is possible that for the elite in French-speaking Africa--and for the masses upon whom they relied for political support--the symbolic rewards of independence such as native rather than foreign rulers, the houses, cars, and emoluments of the white man, the new feeling of individual worth, and the like, constituted sufficient satisfactions during the transition to independence. The sense of efficacy declined, at least for the elite, as post-independence situations undermined the value of the symbolic rewards: the material, tangible benefits of independence proved too often to be intangible, transitory, or too expensive. Moreover, enthusiasm and support, at least for the governing elite (the first-generation respondents) began to erode as it appeared that the "real" benefits of independence were being unequally distributed, and that the problems confronting them before independence remained pressing thereafter. To use Brian Crozier's phrase, they experienced a sort of political "morning after."[32] At least one manifestation of that depression, perhaps, is the _attentisme_, the criticisms, the _desolidarisation_ (a term used by four of the respondents meaning, literally, disengagement) of the second-generation elites. Finally, it may not be too far-fetched to suggest that a significant decline in efficacy may have contributed to an atmosphere of hopelessness in which military coups could be welcomed, even invited, by civilian leaders in Congo-Leopoldville, Dahomey, Upper Volta, the Central African Republic, and Nigeria.

All except three of those who replied to the efficacy question (Questionnaire 2, No. 13) also replied to question No. 14, as did six others who did not reply to No. 13. Question No. 14, phrased in general rather than personal terms, sought to elicit some attitudes about the manner in which effective political competence could be demonstrated. Further, it was hoped that the two questions (No. 13 and No. 14) would give some indication of the extent to which individual respondents had linked their own sense of efficacy to the specific tactics of the politically competent man, that is, one who had a positive evaluation of his ability to manipulate men and political events. A simple tabulation of responses to No. 14 gives the range of priorities assigned to the various alternatives:

(Questionnaire 2, No. 14) "In general, if one wants to influence a governmental decision, the best tactic(s) is (are): (Number in order of importance)."

Alternatives	1	2	3	4	5	6	No Number	Responses
(a) Act through personal or family connections	8	8	2	0	0	2	23	20
(b) Written or telephone communication with government leaders	3	17	15	0	0	1	9	36
(c) Direct communication with government leaders	28	11	2	1	0	0	3	42
(d) Act through political party	7	4	7	6	3	2	15	29
(e) Act through protest demonstration	0	0	1	2	4	2	36	9
(f) Act through group(s) affected by decision	0	2	1	3	3	2	34	11

Other tactics mentioned: inform public, revolution, newspaper articles, public debate, "channels."

These results provide partial confirmation of the conclusions drawn from results of the efficacy questions, at least insofar as they seem to indicate the low order of importance most of the respondents placed on formal or semiformal approaches (alternatives d, e, f). The political party, in most contexts implicitly the dominant party, though given some priority valuation by thirty of the respondents, does not appear to them to be a particularly useful means of solving the influence problem. Other studies have stressed the preference of African leaders for face-to-face political contact,[33] and the results appear to confirm this. Forty-two of the forty-five who answered the question gave alternative (c) some sort of priority, and in fact thirty-nine ranked it first or second. Inescapably, the image of the politically competent man that emerged was one who dealt directly with those in power, be it in a face-to-face situation, by writing, or by telephone. [The ambiguity in alternative (b) is recognized, and probably affected the answers, but not so much as to negate the question, given the large number who chose alternative (c)]. The answers to question No. 14, in this respect, were not unanticipated. Of greater interest, however, was the question of whether individuals with positive or negative senses of efficacy had linked their self-evaluation to the problem of the behavior of the politically competent individual.

On the basis of a breakdown of the responses to the efficacy series (Question No. 13), a rough placement of the respondents along a polarized scale made it possible to dichotomize them as having either a "generally negative" or "generally positive" sense of political efficacy. With the necessary corrections, the respondents to No. 14 who had answered No. 13--separated into thirty-two "generally negative" and seven "generally positive." It appeared that all the "generally negative" respondents had in fact some image of what constituted feasible mechanisms of political competence in their particular circumstances, but it was clear that the fact that they could suggest the best means of demonstrating competence bore little relation to their self-evaluations.

The thirty-two "generally negative" respondents' first priority selections broke down as follows:

Alternatives	Totals
(c) direct communication	15
(a) family and personal	10
(b) written or telephone	4
(d) political party	3

The small number of first-priority selections of alternative (d) in this group (similarly, only one of the "generally positive" group chose (d) as first in importance) tended to support one of the tentative conclusions made with respect to the problem of participation-involvement. The formal political arena--the dominant political party--was not the place where meaningful political changes could be wrought. The "generally negative" group appeared to feel that if change could be brought about, it would be through informal channels, or better still through personal contact with those wielding power. The seven "generally positive" respondents reflected the choices of the "generally negative" group: a preference for the first three alternatives, with (c) the first choice of three of the seven.[34]

It would be hazardous to attempt to account for the lack of linkage between negative self-evaluations and perceptions of what constituted demonstrated political competence. The evidence is too scant for that. One thing is plain, however, and that is the apparent ability of the respondents to compartmentalize what would seem to be mutually conflicting images. They could define the elite to include themselves, then deny that it had any necessary connection with actual influence. They could assess themselves as generally politically incompetent on the national political scene, but still demonstrate that they knew how political influence could be made effective.

V.

THE PAYOFFS OF COMPETENCE, APPRAISALS OF SATISFACTIONS, AND GENERATIONAL CONFLICT

It was suggested earlier that if one of the factors in developing and keeping a positive sense of efficacy is continued satisfactory payoffs, real or symbolic, then most of the respondents, having reached highly valued positions, should have displayed generally positive perceptions of their political competence. This was not the case for most of the respondents who answered the efficacy questions. A highly speculative explanation was offered for the "generally negative" first-generation respondents (see the preceding chapter). But what of the payoffs for the second-generation group? Their generally critical view of their elders, brought out in the discussions on participation and definition of the elite, would seem to point to a widely shared sense of deprivation or failure of symbolic rather than material payoffs. Certainly none of the second-generation respondents, at least insofar as they reported their incomes and present positions truthfully, appeared to be suffering materially (see Appendix A).

The answers to the two questionnaire items on material satisfactions revealed that twenty first-generation respondents declared themselves either "very satisfied" or "satisfied" with their present standard of living, and that eighteen second-generation respondents expressed similar attitudes. ("Niveau de vie," translated "standard of living," was explained in the preliminary interviews as applying to a cumulative evaluation of salary, income, housing, etc.) Asked to look ahead, the two groups varied along lines already suggested by other answers. While only four first-generation respondents saw a negative or unknown material future, fourteen second-generation respondents either saw a reduced living standard or were unsure of the future.

(Questionnaire 2, No. 11) "How satisfied are you with your present standard of living? (Circle the appropriate answer.)"

Alternative	First Generation	Second Generation
I am very satisfied	4	3
I am satisfied	16	15
So-so	5	8
I am not satisfied	2	6
No opinion	4	0

(Questionnaire 2, No. 12) "Do you think your standard of living will improve during the next five years? (Circle the appropriate answer.)

In great measure	2	1
In part	10	7
No change	15	10
Reduction	1	4
No opinion	3	10

On the basis of these replies, it is apparent that most of the respondents in both groups found their material payoffs at least adequate. There was usually no quarrelling with the material benefits of the situation acquise. The two of the first group who expressed dissatisfaction on Question No. 11 revealed the reasons in later discussion: one had not received an alleged perquisite of office, an official vehicle, and the other felt that his official residence was below his expectations.

There was, however, strong dissatisfaction voiced by respondents in both groups about their work and their relationships with superiors and subordinates. Not all the respondents were willing to talk about the extent to which they were satisfied with their jobs or about others with whom they were involved; in all, only forty-seven (twenty-five first, twenty-two second generation) of the sixty-eight who were interviewed consented to do so.

The first-generation respondents who were in government or administration most frequently expressed dissatisfaction with their work. Three themes appeared to pervade their comments:

1. Their work was not sufficiently meaningful, since what they did had no visible effect on improving conditions in the country as a whole. A senior civil servant put it thus:

> One becomes a shuffler of papers (feuilleteur), and one's arm ends in a rubber stamp, not fingers. We feed ourselves, not the people; we promote no one's progress.

2. Their work was frustrating, since what they decided seldom bore any relation to the decisions taken by their superiors on the same matters. (It was interesting to note how often members of both generations used the indeterminate "they" (ils) to identify the object of their grievances.) A guarded and involuted comment by a cabinet minister to this point:

> There are times when the decision of the Party Comité Directeur (Executive Committee) imposes itself upon us, and we have no alternative but to submit. Some of our co-workers are resentful if their finest ideas are not followed or are rejected, but we cannot obviously express our displeasure because to do so would undermine the authority upon which our own authority rests.

3. The lack of cooperation made their work more difficult than it should be. Those who were identified as having either refused cooperation or having given it grudgingly or poorly included, among others, the French technical assistants (mentioned by twelve respondents), higher party cadres (five mentions), lower party cadres (nine mentions), other bureaucrats (ten mentions), religious leaders (three mentions, in Senegal), "foreigners" (six mentions).

A fourth and related theme recurred throughout the discussions with the first-generation respondents, whether in or out of government. This was the perception of pressure and sometimes hostility from younger colleagues and/or subordinates. It is true that some of these comments reflected or even replicated earlier comments made in the discussions on participation, but in this context they became considerably more pointed: "They are jealous of my position and think that they could do a better job in it." "I am not about to submit myself to youngsters whose most important recent experience is the breast of their wet-nurses." "It is true that often they try to sabotage the work of this ministry. But they cannot have responsibility without experience in its management." "They smile, they bow, they say 'Yes, Sir,' but I know that if they could, they would eliminate me from my post. How can one hope to understand such ingratitude?" "We send them abroad so that they can learn to help us. They return believing us all wrong in everything we do, and burning to replace us."

If there was a fairly generalized suspicion of the younger elite on the part of the first-generation group, the second-generation group reciprocated if not in kind, then at least by expressions of hostility and displeasure. As could be expected, members of the younger group tended to be more guarded in their comments and more reluctant to talk about their superiors. Five of the twenty-two in this group saw themselves as "mere *fonctionnaires*," whose primary duty was satisfactory performance of their tasks, and who felt, as a whole, that they enjoyed the trust and favorable disposition of their superiors. Another three were somewhat unsure about their relations with their superiors, but claimed that they had given no cause for dissatisfaction in higher echelons. The remaining fourteen were not only open but highly articulate about a long series of felt grievances relating to their superiors. Almost all, it might be added, referred to the objects of their complaints in the third-person singular or the third-person plural--"il" or "ils"--and in only two cases were specific individuals named. Some representative comments:

> "My views count for little here; if I were older I would be respected."
>
> "Ah, for a few grey hairs! They just don't understand us or our feelings about our work."
>
> "You might as well be talking to the wind when you talk to them. They are so wrapped up in their petty schemes that they have little time to listen to reason."
>
> "My chief is a fine fellow, but a little dense. I find myself running the whole section of this ministry because he is more concerned with his family and house."
>
> "What do you expect when progress is forever held up by time-servers and political sycophants? If I had my way there would be less paperwork and more action."
>
> "The problems with which I deal are not very meaningful. All the important decisions are taken by my superiors. They consult me, but it is just pro forma."

The fourteen shared, it appeared, a feeling that what they were doing was static, that their jobs could become more meaningful if their superiors listened to them more often. They reproached their superiors for unwillingness to try new ideas, for a lack of sincerity in fulfilling obligations, for holding back those with higher qualifications. It was not a question, according to one respondent, of removing "les anciens" from their posts, it was "simply a problem of infusing some vitality into a body grown still long before its time."

However each group felt about the other, or however intensely displeased individuals were about their work, there was no indication that the jobs themselves were being called into question. Only a very small number of all the respondents gave any indications that they would leave their jobs or that they were so displeased that their departure was imminent. The few who indicated they were about to change jobs or seek new work gave promotion, or technical or bureaucratic reasons for the shift. Nor, as was noted earlier, were most of the respondents in the second generation preparing to leap into active party politics.

It became clear, from the picture that began to emerge from preliminary analysis of the satisfaction questions, that one of the reasons why so many of the respondents felt themselves generally inefficacious was that they also had rather negative feelings about their work, and in particular about their relations with subordinates and superiors. At the very least, it appeared the respondents did not feel themselves sufficiently well situated to be able to influence the "real" decision-makers, whoever they were. Their positions were good ones, materially rewarding, valuable enough to be retained and defended against others. What was lacking was a positive feeling about the worth of particular positions and a trust in subordinates and superiors. First-generation elites felt themselves alone, sometimes unable to cope with the problems before them, and given little help by the younger generation. No position, however well rewarded, could long have much relevance under such conditions.

Finally, the question arises whether the respondents' dissatisfaction with non-material factors reflects their true feelings, or whether such dissatisfaction masks desire for change in the material factors as well. There is, of course, no way of knowing what the respondents' "true" feelings were; it is possible that they willfully or unconsciously dissimulated in their responses. They would do so, presumably, to seem more respectable, to rationalize a demand for material gain by veiling it in idealism. The only reply is that it did not appear to the author that the respondents were doing so; to have assumed otherwise the author would have had to question a good deal more of what was said to him during the interviews. This he was not prepared to do.

VI.

THE GENERATIONS AND TWO SETS OF POLITICAL ATTITUDES

Among the more common but undocumented assertions about "older" and "younger" African leaders is that the former reflect a range of "conservative" attitudes associated with domestic developmental priorities, inter-African relations, and international problems. By comparison, "younger" leaders are said to be more "liberal"; that is, to display a greater interest in speeding up and doing more in domestic development, to seek political rather than functional links with other African states, to have a greater interest in closer relations with the USSR and other Communist countries, and to be more preoccupied with such things as the cold war, residual colonialism, and racial matters. Such judgments assume, however one defines "conservative" and "liberal," that there are ostensible differences of attitude between the two groups on most major domestic and international issues. One of our concerns, in the attempt to define the scope of generational conflict within the five countries, was to test this assumption.

The second self-administered questionnaire contained five questions designed to elicit responses about political attitudes along two general dimensions:

1. Perception of international and domestic problems, and their order of priority and magnitude. Question No. 1, completely open-ended except in number of choices, asked for the "ten most important current world political problems." It was assumed that the respondents would not only identify those problems that seemed important to them, but would suggest the salience of the problems by the order in which they were listed. Question No. 6 simply asked for the "most important problems confronting your country," and here the respondents were asked to number their responses according to order of importance.

2. Attitudes about inter-African affairs and relations with other African states, and the modalities of these relations. Here, the questions were phrased to see if the so-called "moderate" versus "radical" dichotomy had any relevance to the respondents. (The "moderates," so called, are supposed to favor functional, gradual steps to achieve African unity, whereas the "radicals," represented by Presidents Nkrumah, Modibo Keita, and Sekou Toure are said to favor rapid or immediate political unification. The "younger" leaders throughout Africa are generally said to favor the "radical" view.)[35] Question No. 2 provided a list of seven alternative directions in which these countries might form "close relations," plus a line for open-ended replies. Within these choices were "buried" two African alternatives that represented the key alternatives in the sense of the whole set of questions. Question No. 3, completely open-ended except for an implied but vague

distinction made in the wording, called for a definition of "pan-Africanism," presumably one of the key terms in the moderate-radical dichotomy. Question No. 4 provided a completely closed choice, with four possible decisions for each item, on seven different inter-African political strategies that envisioned immediate or quick political unification on a regional or trans-African basis and those that provided options for gradual, functional cooperation and integration. It was hoped that the different approaches of the threequestions might provide something of a control on the respondents' consistency.

Before reporting the results of preliminary analysis on the five questions, it must be reiterated that only the questionnaires garnered from Senegal, Upper Volta, Niger, and Dahomey, sixty-three in all, comprise the basis for the analysis. The questionnaires distributed in the Central African Republic were not recoverable, and probably will never be.

Considering the open-ended nature of the question, it was interesting to note the degree of correspondence between the categories cited by both groups and the order of importance of the categories themselves in both sets of responses. One important difference between the two sets is in the number of nominations made: the first generation group developed thirty-seven categories and made 106 nominations; the second generation group cited forty-two categories and made 295 nominations--that is, almost a third more than the first group. Whatever else that fact represents, it does indicate

1. International and Domestic Problems

(Questionnaire 2, No. 1) "In your opinion, what are the ten most important world political problems?"

	First Generation (31)			Second Generation (32)		
Consolidated Rubrics	Order of Importance	Frequency of Nominations	% of total Nominations	Order of Importance	Frequency of Nominations	% of total Nominations
World peace, general international tensions	2	29	14.1	4	34	11.5
Threat of nuclear war	8	13	6.3	7	12	4.0
Colonial questions	6	17	8.3	5	26	8.8
Racial questions	5	18	8.8	6	25	8.5
World economic disparities: rich vs. poor countries	4	19	9.2	3	40	13.6
SE Asia, including Vietnam	1	32	15.5	3	40	13.6
"Yellow peril," Chinese threat	7	15	7.2	9	6	2.0
Assorted non-African non-Asian "hot spots"	2	29	14.1	1	60	20.0
African "hot spots"	3	26	12.1	2	44	14.9
Purely local references	9	8	3.4	8	8	2.7
Totals		206	99.0*		295	99.6*

*Percentages less than 100% due to rounding off.

a much broader, more international set of concerns than were displayed by the first group. Partial confirmation of this lies in the fact that the second group made sixty nominations in the consolidated rubric* "Assorted non-African, non-Asian hot spots," while the first group only made twenty-nine. (The principal categories under this heading, and the number of nominations per group, were Cyprus--I, 2, II, 5; Germany-Berlin--I, 13, II, 18; Arab-Israeli conflict--I, 4, II, 13; UN financial crisis--I, 10, II, 18; Sino-Soviet rift--II, 4; Yemen--II, 1.) Both groups of respondents demonstrated considerable concern for African problems; for the first group these ranked third in importance; for the second group they ranked second. (Categories in this rubric: South Africa, Rhodesia, external interference in Africa, Congo/Leopoldville, inter-African subversion, African unity, aid to Africa, African political development, European-African cooperation. For both groups, the Congo was the important African problem; it received thirteen nominations from the first group, twenty from the second.) Southeast Asia, including the Vietnam situation, ranked high for both groups. It was first in importance for first-generation respondents, (eleven mentions of Vietnam, seventeen mentions of Southeast Asia), and third for the second-generation group (twenty-two mentions of Vietnam, fourteen of Southeast Asia). Similarly, both groups ranked high problems associated with economic disparities between developed and underdeveloped countries,

---

*The consolidated rubrics are arbitrary but logical groupings of categories named by the respondents.

as well as problems coming under the general heading of "world peace and general international tensions." Surprisingly, colonial questions, the threat of nuclear war, and racial problems ranked low in salience for both groups. It is conceivable that given the independence of most of Africa, the present nuclear balance, and the physical distance between the respondents and loci of racial disturbances, these matters no longer have the relevance they might once have had. Of equal interest is the occurrence of nominations under the rubric "yellow peril, Chinese threat." No less than ten of the first generation respondents used the phrase "yellow peril" (le peril jaune); none of the second group did so, although all nine nominations in this group referred to some variant of a "Chinese threat."

The small number of questionnaires makes generalization necessarily hazardous. What can be said, on the basis of what emerges from these data, is that there appears to be little difference, save in emphasis, between the two groups' perceptions of world problems and their salience. Except for a greater emphasis on non-African, non-Asian "hot spot" problems, less preoccupation with the "yellow peril," and a greater emphasis on world economic disparities, the second generation's salience scale virtually replicates that of the first generation.

It was on question No. 6, where the two groups' scale of importance is alike and duplication of concerns would seem to be indicated, that the greatest differences in perception of problems and their salience were actually

(Questionnaire 2, No. 6) "In your opinion, what are the most important problems confronting your country? (Number your answers in the order of their importance.)"

Consolidated Rubrics	First Generation (31)				Second Generation (32)			
	Order of Importance	Frequency of Nominations		% of total Nominations	Order of Importance	Frequency of Nominations		% of total Nominations
Economic problems	1	52	56	54.3	1	50	54	43.5
Financial problems		4				4		
Social problems	3	8		7.7	3	18		14.5
Political problems	2	37		36.0	2	45		36.2
Inter-African relations	4	1		.97	4	6		4.8
Internal subversion	4	1		.97	-	-		--
Modernize army	-	-		--	5	1		.8
Totals		103		99.94		124		99.80

manifested. The difference lay not so much in the priorities assigned to the major rubrics, but in the kind of categories actually named by the two groups. A comparison of the rubric "political problems" as between the two groups bears this out:

First-Generation Respondents		Second-Generation Respondents	
Categories	Frequency of nominations	Categories	Frequency of nominations
Political unity, national unity	12	Political unity, national unity	13
Lack of cadres	11	Political education of masses	9
Lack of responsible leaders	8	Political underdevelopment	11
Corruption	1	Reconversion of mentalities (intellectual underdevelopment)	6
"Decolonisation" of mentalities	1	Lack of cadres	2
Broaden base of party	1	Lack of mass support for regime	1
External African subversion	2	Internal security	1
Continued dependence on France	1		

Though both groups appeared to share almost equal concern with internal political problems--at least insofar as thirty-six percent of the nominations on both sides touched political problems--the differences in emphasis are striking. Whereas the first-generation group assigned primary concern to "political unity" and "lack of cadres" as important problems, the second-generation group stressed a set of nominations that in some respects corresponded to comments they made during the interviews. Many in the latter group, it will be recalled, found fault with their elders for failing to effect "true" changes in the political and economic spheres of their countries, for lacking "dynamism," "vigor," and "initiative." They saw the first generation as protectors of the political status quo, and charged them, consequently, for failing to mobilize potential popular dynamism toward the ends of national construction. The twenty-six nominations in the categories "political education of the masses," "political underdevelopment," and "reconversion of mentalities," would appear to replicate these same concerns.

Both groups demonstrated similar preoccupation with the economic problems of their countries, but the second group showed a greater concern for "social problems" (education, health, population increase, etc.) than did the first.

Lucian Pye, in a well known article,[36] suggested that it was characteristic of political leadership of non-Western countries to be more interested in external than internal problems. Attention to external, global problems had, according to Pye, greater immediate payoffs--in terms of ego-gratification for leaders and generalized support at home--than attention to local problems. A quick comparison of the results derived from the two questions would tend to support his hypothesis. Both groups provided at least twice the number of nominations for the question on world problems that they did for the one on domestic problems. Yet it was with local problems that significant differences in perception developed. It appears that both groups could share generalized perceptions and sets of priorities with respect to world problems, but it was on the matter of local problems--involving more immediate concerns and decisions--that they differed. In any case, the argument for a conservative-liberal dichotomy could not be supported for question No. 1, but could find some support in the results of question No. 6.

It is worth noting that there was significant variation in the patterns of answers as between the countries in only two categories. All of the nominations in the local problems question dealing with internal security, or internal or external subversion, came from Niger, where terrorist attempts by agents of the illegal Sawaba party were still fresh in the minds of respondents.[37] As a matter of fact, while in Niamey, the author himself was an eyewitness--albeit a distant one--to an attempt to assassinate President Hamani Diori of Niger.

2. Inter-African Relations

(Questionnaire 2, No. 2) "Much is currently being said about the future international role of your country. With which world region do you think your country ought to have the closest relations? Second closest? Third? Fourth? (Place the appropriate number after each region.)"

	First Generation									Second Generation								
	Ranking frequencies								Totals as % of Nominations	Ranking frequencies								Totals as % of Nominations
Region	1	2	3	4	5	6	7	Totals		1	2	3	4	5	6	7	Totals	
Europe	6	7	6	2	2	0	0	23	14.4	3	9	7	3	4	1	0	27	17.2
Maghreb states	1	0	0	9	2	1	0	13	8.3	0	1	2	12	2	0	1	18	10.7
North African Arab states	0	1	3	2	3	2	0	11	6.9	1	2	4	5	3	1	1	17	10.1
Sub-Saharan African states	7	11	6	3	1	0	0	28	18.8	7	10	4	2	1	0	0	24	14.2
Eastern Europe and USSR	1	3	2	5	1	3	0	15	9.4	1	0	1	1	5	6	1	15	8.9
French-speaking African states	12	6	7	1	5	0	0	31	19.4	16	6	2	1	0	0	0	25	14.8
Communist China	0	0	1	3	3	3	2	12	7.5	1	1	2	1	3	3	5	16	9.5
Others																		
Africa, general	0	0	0	0	0	0	0	0		1	0	1	1	0	2	1	6	3.5
English-speaking Africa	1	1	2	0	1	1	0	6	3.8	0	0	0	0	0	0	0	0	
United States and North America	0	0	1	6	5	4	1	17	10.7	0	2	4	1	3	1	3	14	8.3
Latin America	0	0	0	0	0	0	0	0		0	0	0	0	0	0	2	2	1.2
Entente	0	0	0	0	0	0	0	0		1	0	0	0	0	0	0	1	.59
Asia, general	0	0	0	0	0	0	1	1	.62	0	0	0	1	0	0	0	1	.59
								157	99.82								166	99.58

(Questionnaire 2, No. 3) "Pan-Africanism" is presently being discussed throughout Africa. Some say that it means--among other definitions--"African unity" or "the union of African states." More precisely, what do you think the term means?

First-Generation Respondents

Rubrics	Frequency
Regional integration, unity by gradual stages	10
Gradual unity through economic cooperation	4
Economic and social cooperation	4
General economic, social and political cooperation	4
Political unity	1
The will to unity	1
Total replies	24

Second-Generation Respondents

Rubrics	Frequency
Regional integration	1
General economic, social and political cooperation	8
Desire for political union	14
Desire for political unity, with affirmation of "African personality"	5
Gradual political union	1
Economic unity	1
Complete elimination of foreign domination	2
Total replies	32

(Questionnaire 2, No. 4) "In particular, are you in favor of or against having your country pursue the following relations with other sub-Saharan African states?"

Policies	For		Against		Undecided		No opinion	
	I	II	I	II	I	II	I	II
a. Political union of French-speaking states with surrender of national sovereignty	12	8	4	14	5	5	2	2
b. Political union of all African states with surrender of national sovereignty	2	9	13	14	6	3	2	3
c. Maintain OCAM*	15	16	1	9	3	0	2	3
d. Establish common financial system	21	28	2	0	0	1	1	2
e. An African common market	19	27	1	0	2	0	1	3
f. An inter-African military force	12	8	2	11	4	6	6	3
g. Creation of regional unions (i.e. west Africa, east Africa, central Africa, etc.) without giving up national sovereignty	19	23	3	3	1	2	0	1

*OCAM: Organisation Commune Africaine et Malagache, created February, 1965.

If the answers to these three questions demonstrated anything, it was that the respondents were not consistent in their attitudes about African unity and its implications. While both groups apparently felt that closer relations with French-speaking Africa, and sub-Saharan African states in general were to be preferred over other directions of relations (the two African alternatives, in both cases, had the highest number of first- and second-rank nominations), they seemed unable or unwilling to spell out those preferences in terms of the standard "moderate-radical" dichotomy. That they had accepted the dichotomy is clear from the responses to the "pan-Africanism" definitional question: eighteen of the first group provided definitions that were gradualist, non-political in orientation, while twenty of the second group gave definitions in which political unity or unification figured. What was interesting is that when confronted with policy choices which specifically pointed in one or the other direction, most indicated preferences considerably at variance with their definitions. The internal consistency of the respondents was checked by comparing the definitions of the eighteen "moderates" in the first group and the twenty "radicals" in the second with their replies to the policy choice question (No. 4). It was assumed that a "gradualist" or "moderate" definition would correspond with favorable selections on items (c) through (g) and unfavorable or undecided selections on items (a) and (b). Conversely, it was expected that "radical" or "political unification" definitions would correspond to negative or undecided selection on items (c) and (g) particularly, with positive selection on items (a) and (b). Only five in the first group and four in the second demonstrated anything like a rough correspondence between their definitions and their policy choices.

There were, in fact, some surprises in the replies to question No. 4. For example, while one-half (twelve) of those in the first group who gave a definition of "pan-Africanism" (twenty-four) selected political union of French-speaking states with surrender of national sovereignty, only two were willing to opt for the same things on an all-African level. Further, more (fourteen) of the second group--whom one would have expected to favor political union with surrender of sovereignty--rejected alternatives (a) and (b) than favored them. On policy (g)--regional unions without loss of sovereignty, twenty-three of the thirty-two second-generation respondents replied favorably, a choice considerably at variance with most of the definitions suggested by them to question No. 3.

In any case, the pattern of responses to the policy question placed most, or a majority of both groups, squarely in the "gradualist" camp.

The inconsistency in the replies can, perhaps, be explained partially by the different levels of the third and fourth questions. The definition question dealt with a politically potent symbol, to which most of the respondents had apparently learned a set response. This was more pronounced in the case of the second group, which included a large number of individuals who had been active in student political groups for which "pan-Africanism" was associated with advocacy of political unity, political integration, anti-colonialism, and the like. The first-generation group, older as a whole than the second group, had learned to respond to the "pan-Africanism" symbol in terms of their countries' involvements in functional African unions and with some degree of skepticism of the "radical" positions taken by such advocates of political union as Nkrumah and Sekou Toure. The point is that the symbol called forth a set response which stood independently of particular applications of the principles implied by that response. Hence, the respondents could divorce the definitions from their implication, and felt free to select among policy choice on heuristic rather than ideological grounds.

VII

CONCLUSIONS

According to J. P. N'Diaye, sixty-three percent of the 294 French-speaking African students in France reached by his survey in 1961 replied that they thought there did, at that time, exist "conflict" between themselves and their respective governments. "Clearly," wrote N'Diaye, "it appears that the reasons for the conflict that pits the students against their governmental leaders stem principally from the decisions taken by these leaders (forty-five percent of the reasons cited). The personal insufficiencies of these leaders that, in some manner, explain their decisions, tallied second (thirty-five percent)."[38] The range of responses in both categories is both interesting and relevant, in light of the results of the present study:

Political Action and Thought[39]	45.0%
1. Betrayed independence--Endorsed neo-colonialist policies--Rejected African unity and solidarity	
2. Favored installation of a bourgeois class--Practiced a ruling class policy against the people and progress	
Personal Qualities	35.0%
1. Lacked personality, general culture, and misunderstood African problems	

2. Corrupt. Seek personal profit and honors

3. Mediocre political background. Lack (political) doctrine. Imprecise political and economic policy line

Aside from the fact that N'Diaye may have gotten a higher percentage of affirmative responses than if he had not asked a somewhat leading question,[*] the charges made by his respondents against their governmental leaders are quite similar in substance to those expressed by many of the second-generation subjects in the present study.[40] The similarity may be purely coincidental, and in fact none of our second-generation group had been involved in N'Diaye's study. On the other hand it is possible that negative political attitudes such as these, learned during student days, may have been carried by the students to their countries of origin and into whatever situations they now find themselves. The persistence of such attitudes might, further, provide some explanation for a good deal of the *attentisme* of youth cited by respondents in both groups. It must be added that since neither our questionnaires nor our interviews touched on this particular point, our data neither confirm nor deny such a hypothesis. In any case, our data do indicate the presence of a good deal of tension, even conflict, between the representatives of the two generations whom we contacted. What are the dimensions of this conflict?

---

[*] N'Diaye's question: "Do you think that there presently exists conflict between your governments and yourselves?" The follow-up question: "If so, what are the causes of it?"

1. <u>A positional dimension</u>. If the data are generalizable, there exists in the five countries of this study, and perhaps elsewhere in French-speaking Africa, fairly widespread discontent focusing upon formal or informal positions of power held by members of the first generation. That discontent is manifested by dissatisfaction over what is perceived as a slow rate of turnover in key positions, as the restrictive nature of recruitment into these positions, and as a narrowing of the channels of promotion and advancement. The targets of that dissatisfaction themselves appear to perceive, in more or less clearly defined terms, a threat from below--particularly from their immediate subordinates. The conflict in this case appears to have nothing or very little to do with formal channels of advancement within the power structures themselves (parties, governments, ministries, etc.) or even with questions of access to key decision-makers. Rather, it seems to involve a vaguely defined sense of mutual hostility held by members of both groups, in which claims to superior wisdom, experience, and legitimacy by the first generation are used to defend their positions against counterclaims of superior expertise, education, skill, and insight by the second. Position in this sense can be a formal office or, more generally, membership in inner circles of decision-making, whether such membership be real or simply imputed. It must be added that the first-generation respondents' defense of their positions was nuanced by their own perceptions that even they, presumably highly placed among the decision-

makers, were able neither to influence satisfactorily the "real" decision-makers nor always to effect decisions satisfactory to them.

2. A policy dimension. The discussions reported in Sections I and II of this preliminary analysis, and the replies to the efficacy questions, all revealed a generalized dissatisfaction with post-independence policy lines and goals on the part of members of both groups, and for different reasons. It was not, it must be stressed, discontent with specific policy decisions or policy lines, but rather a feeling that post-independence policy had in some manner failed to satisfy expectations held by both groups. For the second generation, governmental policies reflected inadequacies of both quality and quantity; there was not enough economic development, leadership was not paying enough attention to public needs, or leadership had blocked or delayed or forestalled constructive policy available through the expertise and superior insight of younger leaders. For the first generation, the right kinds of policies were difficult to obtain because of pressures from below, because of the sheer magnitude of the problems confronting their countries, because "others"--higher up--had failed to see national goals in proper perspective. Both groups, it appeared, had shared high hopes that independence would make pressing economic and political problems more amenable to solutions. And for both groups, a sense that policy-making and its results had not corresponded to their expectations seemed a troubling and frustrating reality.

Neither group, however, appeared willing to see the other given responsibility for making the decisions that might improve the situation, and again, for reasons that had little to do with the policies themselves, but with the personal qualities each group ascribed to the other.

3. A behavioral dimension. The feeling of conflict apparently, if the data are correct, contributed to feelings of alienation and frustration in members of the second generation. These feelings became manifest in such behavior as withdrawal from or rejection of active involvement in party life, verbal rather than participative political activity, *attentisme*, and hyperattention to the technical aspects of their work. Also, for the second-generation group, there appeared to be a willingness to support, even to participate in direct political action to challenge the first-generation powerholders. The attempted coup by Mamadou Dia in Senegal in 1961, for example, had considerable support among young intellectuals, officials, and military leaders.[41] Though Mamadou Dia was still in jail at the time this study was being conducted, seven of the nine Senegalese second-generation respondents mentioned him favorably, or expressed sympathy with what one respondent called Mamadou Dia's attempt to "impose some dynamism, some socialist sense" on Senegalese politics. Further, pro-Dia sentiment is still said to be high among students at the University of Dakar, and if the reports are correct, among Senegalese students in France. The coup that, in October 1963, forced President Hubert Maga out of office and placed Colonel Christophe Soglo

at the head of Dahomey's government, was almost certainly partially engineered by a group of young second-generation elite in the government, the trade unions, and education. For three months, until Soglo voluntarily retired from political power in January 1964, the government was dominated by a group of a dozen or so second-generation technocrats.[42] It is significant that the reappearance of Soglo at the head of the Dahomean government in December 1965, was accompanied by a wholesale housecleaning that again brought a group of technocrats to the fore.[43] The bloodless coup in Upper Volta in January 1966, if the reports are correct, seems to have brought a significant number of the second-generation elite to power.[44] In the Central African Republic, the so-called "young Turks" appeared to have been implicated in some sort of plot against the regime of President Dacko. It was partially to nip this in the bud that Colonel Jean Bedel Bokassa claimed to have seized power on New Year's eve, 1965.[45]

Finally, there is the question of the relationship between the generational discontinuities evident in the five countries studied and the passage to independence. The evidence here admittedly is circumstantial, and any conclusions that can be suggested are highly speculative and tentative at best. Within these terms it can be suggested that independence itself did not represent a <u>causative</u> factor in the conflict between the elite generations, but rather served to define and, perhaps, exacerbate that conflict. To the participants in the elite political culture of French-speaking Africa, independence represented a specific, highly valued goal, an extremely evocative and useful political symbol, and a set of vague but nonetheless real anticipated political payoffs. Crucially, the symbol of independence nurtured diverse expectations, some of which could not be satisfied by the attainment of independence, and nurtured them in both the first- and second-generation elites. To the extent that these expectations--whatever their substance--could not be satisfied, the first-generation leaders adopted defensive attitudes about themselves and their performance as leaders, and to that extent the second-generation leaders could rationalize their opposition to their elders. Independence constituted a convenient focus for the generalized discomfort felt by both groups of leaders.

This study hypothesized the existence of two non-chronological political generations, and, in fact, the selection of respondents and much of the interview questioning assumed that the two groups existed and could be identified. The possibility existed that the division would turn out to be purely artificial, and useful only as an analytical distinction.[46] For that reason, the Senegalese interviews were partially designed to test the hypothesis by specific inclusion of questions that pressed the respondents to clarify their allusions to "youth," "_les anciens_," "the younger generation," "the older generation," and the like. Their statements--and similar statements by respondents in other countries--tended to confirm the hypothesis. The generational allusions had not only a vague chronological referent, but rather specifically defined "generation" in a non-chronological sense. On the one hand the term referred to persons who had reached positions of power before independence, who were part of the original nationalist establishment, and on the other, it referred to people who had come to positions of importance upon independence or shortly thereafter. Independence represented a point of division between the two groups, as did participation in the nationalist groups formed in the period before independence.

The conclusions suggested above, it must be reiterated, are only tentative, and derive only from the data collected. Admittedly, they sometimes go beyond those data when they suggest generalizations applicable elsewhere in French-speaking Africa. In that case, they are not only tentative, but advanced with great caution.

APPENDIX A: THE RESPONDENTS

In order to secure their participation, the respondents in this study were promised complete anonymity. Given the political situations in the five countries visited, the relatively important positions occupied by most of the respondents, and the nature of the questions themselves, this guarantee was deemed necessary. With this reservation, the following is a partial description of the respondents:

1. Occupation. The first-generation group included six legislators (including one Assembly Secretary-General, an appointive administrative post), eleven senior *fonctionnaires* (highly placed officials in executive departments), four ministers of government, one special presidential advisor, four practicing lawyers, two educators (one secondary school teacher, and one secondary school administrator), three labor leaders, one editor of a party newspaper, and one chamber of commerce director, making thirty-six* in all.

The second-generation group included four legislators (two deputies and two Secretaries-General), nine senior *fonctionnaires*, three junion *fonctionnaires*, one special

---

*This figure includes five respondents who were interviewed but did not return the questionnaires. Descriptions in the categories that follow apply only to those who were both interviewed and completed questionnaires.

executive officer, one practicing attorney, six educators (two _lycée_ teachers, two university professors, two secondary school administrators), two professional social scientists, one labor leader, two journalists (one editor, one staff writer), one bank director, one voluntary organization head, and one military officer, making thirty-two in all.

All the respondents were asked to specify the occupation or profession that they undertook immediately after completing their schooling. In thirty cases--particularly, all ten legislators and eight of the twenty senior _fonctionnaires_--this was different from their present occupations. There were, among the sixty-three, twenty-five who had originally been teachers of some sort, fifteen who began as _fonctionnaires_, four attorneys, two journalists, one bank clerk, one soldier, two social scientists, two merchants, two physicians, and one each bank clerk, soldier, planter, draftsman, printer, hydraulic engineer, librarian, machinist, veterinarian, social worker, and housewife.

2. _Education._* The respondents were asked to specify

---

*Inasmuch as a detailed discussion of the equivalence of African-French degrees, diplomas, and certificates to Anglo-American ones is impractical here, simple common descriptive terms are used. No simple equivalents were available for the terms: _licence_, a general degree awarded after two or more years of successful university study in four or five general subject areas; _doctorat_, also known as the _doctorat universitaire_ which is granted to those holding the _licence_ (in most cases), and involves additional studies their highest level of educational attainment. Also, they were asked about degrees, diplomas, or certificates earned, and the identity or location of secondary and higher institutions they attended.

Among the first-generation group were five who had completed only elementary education, fourteen with only secondary educations, four with first-stage baccalaureate, three with second-stage "bacs," four with certificates from technical secondary schools, one with an absolete agricultural proficiency certificate, and two who began but did not finish secondary school, six with university degrees (three licenciés, one doctorat universitaire, two doctorats d'état), one who did not get a university degree but attended three years, two graduates of two of the French grands écoles, one who graduated from a Catholic seminary, one with a medical degree from Dakar, and one with a veterinary medical degree from Dakar.

In the second-generation group, fifteen had only a secondary school education (four bac I, four bac II, four technical certificates, and three other diplomas), fifteen held university degrees (eight licenses, five doctorats universitaires, one doctorat d'état, and one doctorat in preparation), one had graduated from a grande école, and one had a medical degree from France.

---

plus a thesis: the doctorat d'état which is the most difficult to obtain, since it involves two dissertations, both of them enormous and elaborate, plus an oral defense. The last-named degree is seldom completed before a candidate is thirty-five years old.

In all, counting both groups, there were five who had only an elementary school education, twenty-nine with only secondary education, twenty-two with university training, and seven with special higher educational qualifications. Comparing the two groups, the second-generation group contained a larger number of university trained individuals and presented more impressive overall educational credentials than did the former.

3. Age. The range of the aggregate was twenty-five to sixty years of age, and the average age of the respondents was slightly over thirty-seven years. A partial analysis follows:

Group	Median	Mean	Range	Breakdown Within Range	
First Generation	45.0	44.9	34-60	30's:	5
				40's:	20
				50's:	5
				60:	1
Second Generation	33.0	32.8	25-41	20's:	7
				30's:	24
				41:	1

4. Income. By local standards, all of the respondents enjoyed high incomes--at least insofar as they reported them correctly. Most of the respondents did not indicate the extent of their supplemental incomes, but if reports from other sources are to be believed, a considerable number of the elite have incomes beyond their official or regular salaries. These derive--among other sources--

from investments, from the private practice of professions, or, in the case of government employees, from gifts for official services rendered. The last source was said to be a common one in Dahomey, Upper Volta, and the Central African Republic. In any case, reported salaries and incomes were appreciably higher for the first-generation group than for the second; in fact, thirteen of this group reported monthly incomes above 130,000 CFA francs ($537).* Only three second-generation respondents fell into this category. The higher income level of the first group was of course probably due to the fact that the group contained more individuals of higher-ranking position and longer standing on the economic and political scene. With the reservation that of all the data demanded, income reports would be most likely subject to distortion, the results of the income questions are given below:

Range (in francs CFA)	First Generation	Second Generation	US $ Equivalents
50,000 per month	1	6	207 per mo.
60,000 "	3	9	248 "
70,000 "	2	3	289 "
80,000 "	2	2	330 "
90,000 "	6	4	371 "
100,000 "	2	4	412 "
110,000 "	2	0	454 "
120,000 "	0	1	495 "
130,000 "	13	3	537 "

The levels of income by country were, in order from lowest to highest, Dahomey, Upper Volta, Niger and Senegal.

*The exchange rate for the CFA (Communauté Financière Africaine) franc is ca. 242 fr. CFA = $1.00.

5. Interviewees. All those who completed questionnaires were also interviewed. In addition, five interviews were taken in the Central African republic, for which no corresponding questionnaires were obtained. Three of the CAR respondents were *fonctionnaires*, one was a MESAN official, and one was a military officer. The five CAR interviewees were not included in the descriptions given above, but some of the interview materials were utilized in the main text.

APPENDIX B: METHODOLOGY

Five matters will be briefly discussed here with regard to the approach and method of this study: (1) selection of the five countries, (2) selection of the respondents, (3) construction and use of the questionnaires, (4) structure and conduct of the interviews, and (5) special research problems, such as preliminary contact with respondents, interview bias, and the unfavorable circumstances in the Central African Republic.

1. Selection of the five countries. The author had only six months in which to complete the field work for this study, and desired a comparative perspective *within* the political culture of French-speaking Africa. It seemed hopeless to try to visit all the fifteen countries concerned, so it was decided five would provide a rough economic and political sampling for all fifteen. Moreover, it seemed that if the study were to have any generalizable results, the respondents would have to come not only from within the same general political culture, but from representative local variant situations. The fifteen countries were scaled in order of general political and economic development, from most to least advanced in the manner suggested by Russett *et al.* in their *World Handbook of Political and Social Indicators*,[47] with the following result: (1) Ivory Coast, (2) Senegal, (3) Cameroun, (4) Congo/Brazzaville,

(5) Dahomey, (6) Gabon, (7) Malagasy Republic, (8) Guinea, (9) Togo, (10) Upper Volta, (11) Mali, (12) Niger, (13) Chad, (14) Central African Republic, (15) Mauritania. Mali, Guinea, and Congo/Brazzaville were excluded because the American identity of the author and the nature of his study might pose a problem of access in those countries. Malagasy was excluded because of distance. After consulting the scaling results, the calendar, and the airline schedules, Senegal, Upper Volta, Niger, Dahomey, and the CAR were finally selected.

2. Selection of the respondents. The sixty-eight respondents whose attitudes and ideas are reported in this study do not constitute--nor was it intended that they should--a statistically valid sample of the French-speaking African political elite population. (There is, of course, the initial problem of deciding *what* the elite population would be; no generally acceptable definitions or data exist on the subject.) In the aggregate, however, they are significant in that they represented politically relevant strata or groups within each country, and because, by virtue of the positions they occupied, the groups they represented, or their personal attributes, they could and did affect the making of public policy.

The selections were restricted to actors on the modern political scene, since in most of these countries traditional leaders are no longer important except locally. Exceptions do exist, of course, as in Senegal, where the *grands marabouts* wield considerable political influence, and in

Cameroun, where Fulani magnates guarantee the government's political stability in the northern provinces.

The selections were further restricted to actors on the national rather than the local political scene. In the five countries studied, relevant modern political activity tends to be centered in and about the capital city, and tends also to be national rather than local in scope. In effect, given the concentration of wealth, population, and power in the capitals, local politics are national politics. All of the respondents were contacted in the capitals of the five countries. Reasons of economy and schedule prevented contacting potential respondents outside the capitals, as in Upper Volta, where many of the more interesting opponents of former President Yameogo had been dispersed to remote posts in the countryside.

Finally, selections were made on the basis of both positional and reputational criteria. Pre-selection--the compilation of initial lists of about fifty potential interviewees for each country--was made entirely on positional criteria, plus an age factor. (Some 150 or 200 short biographies of leaders in each country were collected during the year prior to the field research, and it was from that collection that the initial lists were compiled). Individuals then occupying important formal positions or offices in government, political parties, trade unions, and education, or visible in intellectual life, or members of the professions were considered likely subjects for the study. After the author arrived in each country, the initial lists were cut down to around thirty. Preliminary investigations in each country suggested additional names of potential respondents, or displaced existing ones. (Changes in position, elimination of offices, the transfer, promotion or demotion of individuals, and sometimes the recent jailing of leaders, had the effect of altering the initial lists.) It must be added that the preliminary in situ investigations were almost indispensable, since the initial lists had been prepared from sources one to three years out of date.

Original plans called for a target of one hundred respondents. Ultimately, only sixty-eight interviews, including sixty-three sets of completed questionnaires, could be obtained.

3. Construction and use of the questionnaires. Two self-administered questionnaires were used for this study, one calling for detailed biographical data and the other, an attitudinal schedule. (See Appendix C.) The rationale behind some of the questions in the latter instrument have been discussed in the body of the study. The questionnaires themselves were intended as the first formal step in the contact with each respondent; the respondents were explicitly asked to complete the schedules before the first interview session, and most were returned to the interviewer at that time. (Eleven sets of schedules were returned to the interviewer by mail after he had left Africa, and three others, all from Dahomey, were not returned at all.) The first contact with the respondents included an explanation of the nature of the study and, if the subject agreed to participate, a discussion

of the questionnaires themselves to clear up any ambiguities in wording or intent.

4. Structure and conduct of the interviews. The interviews usually lasted between one and four hours, depending on the time made available by the respondents. Fifteen of the interviews took two or more sessions to complete. Most of the interviews took place at the offices of the respondents, though some were conducted at their homes, in bars, in restaurants, or some other place picked by the respondents. The structure of the interviews generally varied according to the nature of the respondent, the local political situation, the time available, and the degree to which the interviewer and interviewee established rapport. In any event, the interviewer sought, during each interview, to develop four main themes: (1) definition of the "African elite," including definition of the elite of his own country, and the relationship between the respondent's definition(s) and membership in the dominant party; (2) perceptions of mobility within the elite, definitions of personal political goals, satisfactions with personal mobility, attainment of goals, recognition for achievement; (3) the perceived nature of authoritative decision-making in the respondent's country and his relations thereto; (4) perceptions of the respondent's accountability for personal behavior, and his identifications with various levels of social organization in his particular society. The interviewer developed an outline set of question leads and themes for each country, then sought to use it--with appropriate variations for individual respondents--

throughout his stay in that country. The author has to admit he was not always completely successful in being able to follow his outlines. Finally, all the interviews were conducted in French, though several of the respondents would have liked to practice their English on the author.

5. Special research problems. The field research for this study was undertaken during the period January to May, 1965. It had been hoped that preliminary contact with most of the potential respondents might be possible before the author left for Africa, in order to set up priority lists and assure the cooperation of particularly important respondents. To determine whether such preliminary contact might be feasible on a large scale, a test mailing of twenty letters to potential Dahomean respondents was made in the spring of 1964. Each letter, which explained the proposed nature of the study and solicited the addressee's participation, was sent together with an airmail envelope addressed to the author and stamped with appropriate Dahomean postage. By October, only one reply had been received from Dahomey, and that from the secretary of a respondent, who indicated that her employer had not been in his office for three weeks. (When asked later, five of the Dahomean respondents acknowledged having received the letter, and regretted not having answered it.) The results of the sample mailing, it need hardly be added, discouraged further attempt at preliminary contact.

Another problem, certainly not new to such research, arose out of the interview situation. This was the problem of interview bias, particularly crucial here, where the national identity of the researcher might evoke negative attitudes and where the professional interests of the interviewer were susceptible to misunderstanding and misinterpretation. The last-named difficulty was to some extent mitigated by avoiding the term "political science," which most respondents had either never encountered in its American sense or tended to equate with political advocacy, and by substituting "political sociology" whenever possible. ("Sociology" apparently fitted into a cognitive pigeonhole familiar to most respondents, while "political science" did not.) The national identity of the interviewer did prove a problem for four contacts, who specifically refused to participate in the study because they said they didn't like Americans, and in particular, American professors. Otherwise, the fact that the interviewer was an American did not appear to affect the conduct of the interviews or the kinds of responses given. Once contact had been established, the author usually found little trouble in establishing a level of rapport sufficiently close to permit a satisfactory interview. To round out the record, in all some 137 potential respondents were contacted; thirty-five in Senegal, twenty-seven in Upper Volta, twenty-nine in Niger, forty in Dahomey, and twenty-six in the CAR. Unsuccessful attempts were made to contact another thirty. Most of the refusals involved the potential respondents' heavy schedules, pressure of work, imminent departure or return, other commitments, and the like. About twenty persons contacted felt that because of their positions they could not become involved in a study that had political overtones.

Finally, there were the author's problems in the Central African Republic. Written authorization to pursue the study was first obtained from the Ministry of Foreign Affairs and other appropriate governmental agencies, and then some twenty-six potential respondents were contacted by the author. For reasons never explained, the author's permission to conduct the research was subsequently revoked, he was followed, interrogated at length by the police about his intentions and work, his respondents were contacted and apparently warned to have no more to do with him, his personal effects were searched, and as he was leaving Bangui, his effects were again searched and various papers and documents (including one completed set of questionnaires and a list of respondents) were confiscated. At no time were formal charges made against the author, but it became clear that for reasons known only to the CAR government, he would not be permitted to conduct his study in that country. The author left with only five partially completed interviews, his notebooks, and no completed questionnaire forms. (The notebooks were probably not confiscated because they were illegible, having been written in the author's private variety of shorthand.)

APPENDIX C: QUESTIONNAIRES

(Translated from the French)

Project EFSA
Washington University

QUESTIONNAIRE 1

Case No. ___________ _______________ (Date completed)

1. Date of birth ______________________
2. Place of birth (specify town, department, region, etc.)
____
3. Ethnic affiliation /coutume ou ethnie/ ______________________
4. Religious affiliation (circle appropriate item)
   - Protestant (specify sect) ______________
   - Muslim
   - Catholic
   - Other (specify) ______________________
5. Marital status (circle appropriate item)
   - Divorced
   - Bachelor (single)
   - Monogamous
   - Polygamous (no. of wives) __________
6. Trade or profession of father (circle appropriate item)
   - Farmer /cultivateur/
   - Stockherder
   - Planter
   - Merchant
   - Civil servant
   - Teacher
   - Physician
   - Lawyer
   - Minister (religious)
   - Traditional chief
   - Other (specify) ______________ ______________ ______________
7. At what (educational) level did your father end his studies? __________
8. How many people reside presently with you? __________
9. What language or dialect is spoken in your home, for the most part?
____
10. Your education (circle appropriate items)

Level	Years completed	Certificates, brevets, diplomas, etc.
Primary	1 2 3 4 5 6	CEP, (Other) ______________
Secondary	1 2 3 4 5 6 7	BAC1 BAC2 BEPC BE BEC (Others) ___
Technical	1 2 3 4 5 6 7	BEPC BE BEC BEI (Others) ________
University	1 2 3 4 5 6 7	Bachelor Licence Doctorate (Others) ____________

QUESTIONNAIRE 1, p. 2

Case No. ____________

11a. Other schools (grandes écoles, etc., specify)

____

11b. Names, locations, of secondary schools where you studied, with inclusive dates ____

____

____

11c. Names, locations, of higher educational institutions (universities, etc.) where you studied, with inclusive dates ____

____

____

____

11d. If you obtained a doctorate, please give name of institution, date the degree was awarded, and title of thesis or theses ____

____

____

12. What trade or profession did you choose to pursue after you finished your studies? ____

____

12a. What is your present occupation? ____

____

12b. How long have you practiced your present trade or profession? ____________

____

13. Occupational history (in reverse chronological sequence).

Short description of work	Employed by	Inclusive dates

If you need more space, please use the reverse of this page.

QUESTIONNAIRE 1, p. 3

Case No. __________

14. Amount of your present salary (in CFA francs per month; please circle the appropriate item)

less than 50,000	90 - 99,999
50 - 59,999	100 - 109,999
60 - 69,999	110 - 119,999
70 - 79,999	120 - 129,999
80 - 89,999	130,000 and above

15. Are you engaged in another occupation (trade, profession, commerce, etc.) and/or do you own income property? If yes, please estimate your yearly supplementary income from these sources:

____

16. Your membership in trade unions, associations, political parties, etc.. Do you now hold or have you ever held a responsible position or office in any of these organizations?

Name of organization	Dates of membership	Position or Office

If necessary, use the reverse of this page.

QUESTIONNAIRE 2

Project EFSA
Washington University

Case No. ____________

____
(Date Completed)

1. In your opinion, what are the ten most important world political problems?

____
____
____
____
____
____
____
____
____
____

2. Much is currently being said about the future international role of your country. With which world region do you think your country ought to have closest relations? second closest? third? fourth? (place the appropriate number after each region).

Western Europe ____________
Maghreb states ____________
North African Arab states ____________
Eastern Europe and USSR ____________
French-speaking African states ____________
Communist China ____________
Others (specify) ____________
____

3. "Pan-Africanism" is presently being discussed throughout Africa. Some say that it means--among other definitions--"African unity" or "the union of African states." More precisely, what do you think the term means?

____
____
____

QUESTIONNAIRE 2, p. 2

Case No. __________

4. In particular, are you in favor of or against having your country pursue the following relations with other sub-Saharan African states:

	For	Against	Undecided	No opinion
a. Political union of French-speaking states with surrender of national sovereignty				
b. Political union of all African states with surrender of national sovereignty				
c. Maintain OCAM				
d. Establish common financial system				
e. An African common market				
f. An inter-African military force				
g. Creation of regional unions (i.e., west Africa, east Africa, etc.) without giving up national sovereignty				

5. During the next five years, who are the African leaders who, in your opinion, will play the most important roles in inter-African politics? (Indicate by No. 1 the most important; by No. 2, the second, and so on.)

____

____

6. In your opinion, what are the most important problems confronting your country? (Number your answers in the order of their importance.)

____

____

____

____

____

____

QUESTIONNAIRE 2, p. 3

Case No.____________

7. Generally speaking, who, in your opinion, are the ten most influential people in your country?

____

____

____

____

____

8. More precisely, who are the five most influential people in each of the following social categories:

Government, Administration	Commerce	Trade Unions	Political Party(ies)

1. ______________________________
2. ______________________________
3. ______________________________
4. ______________________________
5. ______________________________

Others (with short identification, please) ____________

____

II.

9. When you finished your studies, what trade or profession did you wish to pursue? ____________

10. If you are now engaged in an occupation <u>different</u> from the one you name in Question No. 9, why did you make the change?

____

____

11. How satisfied are you with your present standard of living? (Circle the appropriate item.)

I am very satisfied

I am satisfied

So-so

I am not satisfied

No opinion

Case No. ___________

12. Do you think that your standard of living will improve during the next five years? (Please circle the appropriate item.)

In great measure

In some measure

No change

Reduction

No opinion

13. Suppose the national government is considering a law that you judge to be unjust or pernicious. What do you think you could do about it?

____

____

____

a. In such a situation, what are the chances that you would do something to show your opposition?

____

b. If you do make an effort to change the law, what are the chances that you might be successful in your efforts?

____

14. In general, if one wants to influence a governmental decision, the best tactic(s) is (are): (Number in order of importance.)

________ Act through personal or family connections

________ Written or telephone communication with governmental leaders

________ Direct communication with governmental leaders

________ Act through political party

________ Act through protest demonstration

________ Act through group(s) affected by decision

Other tactics: ____

____

____

NOTES

1. James S. Coleman and Carl G. Rosberg, Jr., _Political Parties and National Integration in Tropical Africa_ (Berkeley: University of California Press, 1964), p. 673.

2. In addition to the respondents, the author sought out a wide variety of other persons in order to obtain background material. Among them were diplomats, journalists, social scientists, and administrators from a dozen countries stationed in the five states visited.

3. The idea is implicit in Ruth Schachter Morgenthau's _Political Parties in French-Speaking West Africa_ (London: Oxford University Press, 1964), and Immanuel Wallerstein's "Elites in French-Speaking Africa: The Social Basis of Ideas," _The Journal of Modern African Studies_, No. 1 (1965), pp. 1-33.

4. Wallerstein, _op. cit._; Thomas Hodgkin, _Nationalism in Colonial Africa_ (London: Frederick Muller, 1956), pp. 169-184; Thomas Hodgkin, "A Note on the Language of African Nationalism," in Kenneth Kirkwood, (ed.), _African Affairs_ (St. Antony's Papers No. 10, [London: Chatto and Windus, 1961]), pp. 22-40.

5. Morgenthau, _op. cit._, pp. 12-13, 18-20; Virginia Thompson and Richard Adloff, _French West Africa_ (London: George Allen and Unwin, 1958), pp. 523-526.

6. J(ean)-P(ierre) N'Diaye, _Enquête sur les étudiants noirs en France_ (Paris: Editions Réalites Africaines, 1962).

7. Wallerstein, _op. cit._, _passim_. Hodgkin, "A Note...," _op. cit._

8. The fullest discussion of the role of trade unions in the rise of nationalism in French-speaking Africa is to be found in Jean Meynaud and Anisse Salah-Bey, _Le syndicalisme africain_ (Paris: Payot, 1963). See also the bibliography on African labor on the back page of the June, 1965, issue of _Africa Report_, which also contains some excellent articles on the subject.

9. Morgenthau, _op. cit._, _passim_; Thompson and Adloff, _op. cit._, pp. 83-107; André Blanchet, _L'Itineraire des partis africains depuis Bamako_ (Paris: Plon, 1958); Ernest Milcent, _l 'A.O.F. entre en scene_ (Paris: Bibliothèque de l'Homme d'Action, 1958); Léo Hamon, "Introduction à l'étude des partis politiques de l'Afrique française," _Revue juridique et politique d'outre-mer_, No. 2 (1959); Léo Hamon, "Le Parti Fédéral Africain et le Rassemblement Démocratique Africain: de la querelle fédérale à l'indépendance (1959-1960)," _Revue juridique et politique d'outre-mer_, No. 3 (1961), pp. 337-353; Phillipe Decraene "L'Evolution des partis politiques en Afrique au Sud du Sahara," _Civilisations_, No. 12 (1962), pp. 196-206.

10. For example, the old ties of the RDA were cited by President Houphouet-Boigny as one of the rationales for the continued existence of the Conseil de l'Entente, and indeed, for its revival in 1964. See Pierre Biarnes' "Note mensuelle

de conjoncture," _Moniteur africain de commerce et de l'industrie_ (Dakar, January, 1965).

11. Max Gluckman, _Custom and Conflict in Africa_ (Oxford: Basil Blackwell, 1959), pp. 27-53.

12. Professor James S. Coleman makes the point thus: "Rapid and fundamental transformation in social structure and power relationships is bound to make the problem of elite succession acute, unpredictable, and highly visible. When an essentially static society marked by widespread illiteracy and a predominance of ascriptive criteria moves toward a dynamic and modernizing society where education is the principal criterion of upward mobility and stratificational position, each successive wave of better educated persons presents a challenge to its predecessor." James S. Coleman, (ed.), _Education and Political Development_ (Princeton, New Jersey: Princeton University Press, 1965), p. 358. The literature on generational conflict is not extensive; see Suzanne Keller, _Beyond the Ruling Class: Strategic Elites in Modern Society_ (New York: Random House, 1965), pp. 246-251; Douglas E. Ashford, "Second and Third Generation Elites in the Maghreb," (Policy Research Study, U.S. Department of State, Washington: 1964); and, in broader sociological context with an emphasis on adolescents, see S. N. Eisenstadt, _From Generation to Generation_ (Glencoe: The Free Press, 1965). A loosely connected group of essays on generational conflict was collected in the only French work of any note on the subject: _Les conflits de générations_. (Paris: Presses Universitaires de France, 1963). The

collection was probably edited by Jean Darcet, though he is not listed as editor. Pp. 23-55 discusses the problem in relation to French-speaking Africa, but without reference to any specific writing or research.

13. Professor Morgenthau explicitly recognized this point and stated that her book was "mainly about the work of the first generation, the 'founding fathers' of the parties and the new states." _op. cit._, pp. xxi-xxii.

14. This point is made exceedingly well by Michael Crowder in his "Independence as a Goal in French West African Politics" in William H. Lewis, (ed.), _French-Speaking Africa, The Search for Identity_ (New York: Walker and Company, 1965), pp. 15-41.

15. _International Social Science Bulletin,_ VIII (1956), pp. 413-24. The summary is by J. E. Goldthorpe, "Education and Social Change," in Aidan Southall, (ed.), _Social Change in Modern Africa_ (New York: Oxford University Press, 1961), p. 147. The literature on elites is extraordinarily extensive. Two useful bibliographies dealing with African elites are: William J. and Judith L. Hanna, _Politics in Black Africa: a selective bibliography of relevant periodical literature_ (African Studies Center, Michigan State University, 1964), pp. 76-81; and Carl Beck, _et al._, _A Survey of Elite Studies_ (Washington, D. C.: Special Operations Research Office, The American University, 1965), pp. 64-65. Wallerstein's paper _op. cit._ also contains a useful bibliography. A selective bibliography "Youth Groups and Young Leaders in the Developing Countries,"

(Bureau of Intelligence and Research, U. S. Department of State, July 1964) is also of interest. A recent, useful compendium of studies on African elites drawn from papers presented at the Sixth International African Seminar at the University of Ibadan, Nigeria, in 1964, is: P. C. Lloyd, (ed.), The New Elites of Tropical Africa (New York: Oxford University Press, 1966).

16. The distinction is discussed in and the quotation drawn from S. N. Eisenstadt, "Changes in Patterns of Stratification Attendant on Attainment of Political Independence," Transactions of the 3rd World Congress of Sociology (London: 1956), III and IV, p. 36.

17. Wallerstein, op. cit., passim; the quote is from an earlier version of this article.

18. Aiden Southall, "Traditional Structure and the Formation of Elites in East Africa" (Paper presented at African Studies Association Annual Conference, October 1965), p. 3.

19. These observations are drawn from the author's unpublished notes, taken in the Cameroon, Senegal, and other West African states during 1960 and 1961.

20. For a general discussion of the conditions for the creation of engagé militants, see Seydou Badian, Les Dirigeants africains face à leur peuple (Paris: François Maspero, 1964), pp. 97-117.

21. P. Mercier, "Evolution of Senegalese Elites," International Social Science Bulletin, VIII, No. 3 (1956), pp. 441-452; Morgenthau, op. cit., pp. 125-165, passim;

Michael Crowder, Senegal: A Study in French Assimilation Policy (London: Oxford University Press, 1962); William Foltz, "Senegalese Political Parties," in James S. Coleman and Carl G. Rosberg, (eds.), Political Parties and National Integration in Tropical Africa (Berkeley: University of California Press, 1964), pp. 16-64.

22. Morgenthau, op. cit., p. 11.

23. There are no hard data on the number of such individuals; the author was given several figures by responsible government sources; in 1964, according to one source, there were over 900 applications for 83 positions open in government administration. There was no way to verify this. What is apparent is the pull of the urban centers upon the educated Senegalese, and the equally strong pull of governmental work for these individuals. An official report of a questionnaire sample survey of 1,000 rural secondary school graduates who had completed their schooling in 1954 indicated that five years later three-fourths had moved to urban areas, three-fourths had undertaken so-called "intellectual" occupations (teachers, civil servants), and only two percent had remained rural in occupation and residence. Rapport Général sur les Perspectives de Développement du Sénégal, 2nd ed. 1963, (Republic of Senegal, Ministry of Planning, Development and Cooperation, part I, pp. 1-5 [19]). The same document later (pp. 1-7 [19]) suggests reasons for the pull exercised by government work (translation mine):

> Generally, the most prestigious occupation in the eyes of Senegalese, particularly if they have attained a minimum of culture, is the profession of fonctionnaire: that which tempts young Senegalese in the profession of fonctionnaire is, essentially, the promise of security.

24. *Moniteur africain de commerce et de l'industrie* (Dakar) No. 174, January 30, 1965, p. 2.

25. *Statistiques Scolaires*, 1963-1964 (Republic of Upper Volta, Ministry of National Education, Ouagadougou: 1964).

26. Virginia Thompson, "Dahomey," in Gwendolen Carter, ed., *Five African States* (Ithaca: Cornell University Press, 1963), p. 196.

27. *Mémento de l'économie africaine au sud du Sahara, 1965* (Special number of *Bulletin de l'Afrique Noire*, No. 354, 1964: [Paris, Ediafric, 1964]), p. 186.

28. For a discussion of the concepts associated with efficacy, political competence, civic competence, see Gabriel Almond and Sidney Verba, *The Civic Culture* (Princeton University Press, 1963), pp. 180-184. Applications are discussed in the same work, pp. 184-257 ff.

29. *Ibid.*, pp. 528-529 (Questions 22-30).

30. The respondents often noted this themselves. My own research in Cameroun before independence (1959 and 1960) indicated this as well. See Victor T. LeVine, *The Cameroons, From Mandate to Independence* (Los Angeles: University of California Press, 1964), pp. 215-218.

31. Elisabeth Colson, "Competence and Incompetence in the Context of Independence," to be published during 1967 in *Current Anthropology*.

32. Brian Crozier, *The Morning After* (London: Methuen, 1963).

33. See, for example, W. J. M. Mackenzie and Kenneth Robinson, (eds.), Five Elections in Africa (Oxford: The Clarendon Press, 1960).

34. A commentator on this study raised the perfectly valid point that "party activity can give you a position of authority because it puts you in touch with the Minister," questioning (by implication) the rejection of party by some of the respondents as a favored channel of political influence. This would be true if in fact party membership permitted one to do so. Yet, there is evidence that internal cleavage within political parties may discourage the use of party channels for communication in these countries; indeed, it may incur obligations to the party (not just to the Minister) that the initiator of the contact might wish to avoid. Moreover, most of the respondents in this study were so situated that they would not need party channels to effect communication. The commentator also suggests that the "negative self-evaluations" described in the study would probably not hold for similarly placed individuals in white Rhodesia, and that "much depends on the individual's reputation for technical competence." This may well be true--there are, at least, no data to the contrary. But this study did not deal with such individuals, nor was it intended to do so. The point about technical competence is well-taken, but our data do not support it. A number of the respondents with "negative self-evaluations" were in fact men (and women) with undoubted high levels of technical competence. This fact did not, however, prevent them from feeling that their expertise was

often lost on their superiors, that the latter often made decisions on "purely political" (i.e. non-rational) rather than technical grounds.

35. The dichotomization of African leaders' views on the subject of inter-African relations is best covered in Colin Legum, Pan-Africanism, 2nd ed. (New York: Praeger, 1965). See also Victor D. DuBois, The Search for Unity in French-Speaking Black Africa, (American Universities Field Staff Reports, West Africa Series, Vol. VIII, Nos. 3, 4, 5, 6. New York [1965]). Report No. 6, entitled "Relations Between the 'Moderate' and the 'Revolutionary' States: The Case of Guinea," is particularly in point.

36. Lucian W. Pye, "The Non-Western Political Process," Journal of Politics, Vol. XX (August, 1958), pp. 468-486.

37. The Sawaba is discussed in Franz Ansprenger, Politik im Schwarzen Afrika (Koeln and Opladen: Westdeutscher Verlag, 1961), pp. 358-360. A discussion of the Sawaba and its Communist Chinese connections is "Un cas d'intervention chinoise en Afrique occidentale: le Niger," Le Monde (Paris) February 4, 1965, p. 6. See also the comments and description of Sawaba "guerilla fighters handbooks" in Gilbert Comte, "Les Carnets de Nanking," Est et Ouest (Paris) No. 357, 1966.

38. N'Diaye, op. cit., p. 223.

39. Loc. cit.

40. Similar attitudes were found among students at the University College of Nigeria at Ibadan by William John Hanna in 1960. The report of his questionnaire survey is published in Coleman and Rosberg, op. cit., pp. 413-443; the opinions in point are reported on pp. 432-441.

41. The most extensive discussion of the Mamadou Dia affair is by Victor D. DuBois in a three-part series, The Trial of Mamadou Dia, (American Universities Field Staff Reports, West Africa Series, Vol. VI, Nos. 6, 7, 8 [1963]). No. 6, "Background of the Case," is relevant because it describes, to some extent, the basis of Mamadou Dia's support.

42. This fact has not, as far as I am aware, been documented publicly. Given my promises to my respondents, several of whom were involved in this group, their anonymity must be maintained, at least for the present.

43. Colonel Soglo's new government included nine Ministers and one High Commissioner. Two Ministers are physicians (Emile Zinsou, Foreign Minister, and Daouda Badara, Public Health), one an engineer (Marcel Dadjo, Transport, Posts and Telecommunication), one an economist (Nicophere Soglo, Finance and Economic Affairs), one the former director of SONADER, the state corporation for rural development (Moise Mensah, Rural Development and Cooperation), one former teacher (Eugene Boce, National Education, Youth, and Sports), and the rest, professional administrators or technicians (Arsene Kinde, Justice and Legislation; Pascal Chabi Kao, Civil Service; Christian

Vieyra, High Commissioner for the Plan and Tourism). Stanislas Adotevi, a former teacher and young intellectual, became Secretary-General of Government. Afrique Nouvelle (Dakar) No. 900, week of December 30, 1965-January 5, 1966, p. 5.

44. See Afrique Nouvelle, No. 962, week of January 13-14, 1966, pp. 5 and 16. Simon Kiba's three-part report on the Upper Voltan coup emphasizes the role of discontent among the younger elites; see Afrique Nouvelle, No. 965, week of February 3-9, 1966; No. 966, week of February 10-16, 1966; No. 967, week of February 17-23, 1966.

45. Colonel Bokassa claimed that he had discovered plans to set up a so-called "People's Army," to be trained by the Chinese or their supporters. The "Army's" general staff allegedly included Messrs. Nzallat, chief of the political office in President Dacko's staff, and Mounounbai, head of state security. Le Monde (Paris) January 8, 1966, p. 6. Both Nzallat and Mounounbai were said to have been among the "Young Turk" group in the CAR government, known for its radical views and favorable attitudes to the Chinese communists.

46. James S. Coleman, in Education and Political Development, op. cit., p. 358, distinguished between three political generations: (1) traditional elites, (2) "the first wave of modern educated elites," and (3) "the succeeding generation of better educated and professionally more qualified persons." He described the latter group as a "post-revolutionary generation of technicians and managers."

47. Bruce Russett *et al.*, *World Handbook of Political and Social Indicators* (New Haven: Yale University Press, 1964) pp. 293-303.